Santa Muerte: Altars, Offerings Prayers, & Spells

Marta Sevilla

CONTENTS

INTRODUCING SANTISIMA MUERTE

Santisima Muerte is known by a number of other names including Santa Muerte (Holy Death)

Senora de las Sombras (Lady of the Shadows)
La Flaca (The Skinny One)
Nina Santa (Holy Girl)
Senora Blanca (White Lady)
Senora Negra (Black Lady)
Senora Rojo (Red Lady)
La Calaca (The Skeleton)
La Santisima (Most Holy)
Blanquita (Little White Girl)
La Nina Blanca (The White Girl)
Dona Sebastiana (Lady Sebastianne)
Senora de la Noche (Lady of the Night)
La Huesuda (The Bony One)
And these are only a few that she goes by.

To those that follow her, Santa Muerte is believed to be a saint, although she is not recognized by the Catholic Church. She's actually banned of recognition. So why would devout Catholics and Christian followers continue to pray to her? There are probably as many answers to this question as there are Christian followers. I can only speak from what I have been told by others who are Santa Muerte devotees and my own beliefs on the subject.

I know many people who work very closely with Santa Muerte, myself included. When I have posed this same question to these people I got some very interesting answers.

Some say that they simply don't believe that she is evil. Yes, Santa Muerte will and does answer dark requests and petitions but it's up to the person working with her. If the practitioner does not make a dark request then they are not working evil magic. Santa Muerte does not separate good and evil. There is no distinction between the two in her eyes. Petitions are just that.....petitions, cries for help in times of need. The distinction between good or evil workings is in the eye of the spellworker or petitioner. No person is ever forced to work the darker side of the art. Santa Muerte is just as happy to answer good requests as well as the dark ones. She is happy to perform healing miracles, grant money wishes, or help a person find employment. Others have expressed their belief that Santa Muerte is the deceased version of the Virgin Mary, particularly the Virgin of Guadalupe. The Holy Virgin seen without the beautiful toned skin. She is seen as she should look after years and years of death and decay. Bones. Therefore, being the Holy Mother herself, they treat her with love, devotion, and with the highest respect. To them Santa Muerte is Holy.

Some of these people go on to explain their desire to be on the good side of both the Holy Saints in Heaven and the Saint of Death. Death is a subject that is viewed differently by everyone. These people pray to God, Saints, and Angels. This is done so that they are on their good side and enjoy the gifts of health and happiness while still in the living. But they also want to stay on the good side of Santa Muerte, the saint of death, in order to be looked upon kindly when death comes knocking at their own door. They believe that Santa Muerte can and will provide them with "a good death". A death without suffering and pain. Death can come at any time so these people feel that by being on the good side of both they will be well equipped for anything that comes their way.

And still others pray to Santa Muerte because they believe that she will grant favors that other Saints will not grant. She will respond to requests of any nature and will never cast judgment upon a person for asking or what they ask for. Some Saints will not grant request of money, splitting up a couple's relationship, taking revenge on an enemy, causing harm, or sexual encounters. Santa Muerte on the other hand will.

Santa Muerte accepts everyone alike. There are no rules. You don't have to live a certain way of life or believe in a certain set of standards. I have read many articles claiming that only those who are criminals, drug dealers, rapists, molesters, and any other law-breakers work with Santa Muerte. This is far from the truth. Her following comes in all forms and from all walks of life.

There are many doctors, nurses, housewives, carpenters, young and old, rich and poor, male or female who work with her. It's not just the law-breakers who turn to Santa Muerte as these articles claim.

The beauty of working with Santa Muerte is that she is a complete and total magical system in herself. This means that she can be called upon for every single need a person may have. Unlike the Saints and other deities who can only be called upon for issues that are within their particular workings or patronage, Santa Muerte has no limits or restrictions. A person doesn't even have to work with her on a routine basis to receive her help. Many work with her in conjunction with working with Saints and other deities.

Another misconception is that Santa Muerte will take revenge on those who fail to fulfill their promises to her. Or that she will claim the life of a family member in return for granting a request made to her. This is also a myth. Santa Muerte will not make punishment for granting favors asked of her, nor for the lack of fulfilling promises made. Although I won't advise that a person not fulfill their promise. This is only because if they ever need her help again in the future she will not listen nor help.

It's believed that Santa Muerte is rooted way back to the Aztecs, particularly to the goddess Mictlancihuatl, the goddess of death and the wife of Mictlantecuhtli who together ruled over the world of the dead and the underworld. Interestingly, the spider, the owl and the bat are associated with him as they are with Santa Muerte. Because she is known as the Lady of the Dead, and for other similarities, she and Santa Muerte are considered one in the same.

In the Aztecs viewed death as the continuation of life. They believed that at the time of death the person's soul went to one of three separate places. Those that passed away in battle, woman that passed away during childbirth, and all the ritually sacrificed ones would go straight to the realm of the Sun God, Huitzilopochtli. Those who passed away by drowning, thunderstorms, hit by lightning, or in connection with festering wounds would go to the place that was ruled by the Rain God. Those who passed away by natural causes went to Mictlan. But before the soul would reach Mictlan it would first have to go through the nine lives of the underworld before reaching their final destination. There in Mictlan was the ruler and co-ruler Mictlantecuhtli and Mictlancihuatl.

Mictlantecuhtli has been described as a bloody skeleton figure. He wore necklaces made of human bones and his clothing oftentimes were adorned with bones, teeth and eyeballs.

Mictlancihuatl was viewed in much the same way. In the ancient Aztec culture skeletons and bones were viewed differently than they are today. The Aztecs seen them as symbols of fertility, health, and abundance.

Death was an important part of life to the Aztecs, an extension into another world. Life went on even after death. The dead were never forgotten. Instead they were honored and invoked. They held special rituals in honor of the deceased which is where, in my opinion, started the feast of Day of The Dead. They believed that forty days after a persons death the spirit would return.

THE THREE ROBES OF SANTA MUERTE

If you shop around long enough you will find several different variations of statuary and imagery. Some statues may or may not show Santa Muerte holding a scythe. Some include an owl, a globe, scales, or an hour glass. I have even seen her image with angel wings. Sometimes parts of the statue are removable. These can be purchased in plastic, ceramic, cement, resin, carved from wood and either left as they are or filled with magical items.

She appears as the grim reaper, an image of a skeleton who always seems to look alive. Various colors are also available. Each of the different colors has a particular meaning and use. Selecting one is a matter of personal preference. The size of the image isn't as important as the color selection. It doesn't matter whether the image is a large and elaborate table size representation or a small pocket size representation. They all work in the same way.

There are three basic colors used when working with the Santa Muerte. These are red, white, and black. When working with Santa Muerte these are the only three colors needed. Everything that is not mentioned under the black or red image is used for working with the white image. There are also other special colors that can be obtained and are very good to work with. So let's explore the color associations and how they are used.

LA BLANCA-WHITE IMAGE

Representations in WHITE are commonly used to clear away negative energies around us, around our homes, businesses, and environment. This color is for purification and to remove obstacles from a person path. These would be obstacles which keep the practitioner from making spiritual or life progress, reaching goals, and amplifying their ambitions. It's also used to clear away negative mental emotions. While some of the other colors can be used, the representation in white is similar to being "all purpose".

Being a color that deals with some of the humanly emotions the white statue is often employed for counteracting the effects of grudges, hate, hurt feelings, envy, jealousy, anguish, and disputes. In addition, her white image can be used in healing rituals and spellwork or give someone motivation, courage, or to overcome fears.

The white representations is also protective. Protection from enemies, protection from evil, protection from mishaps, protection from harm, protection from false friends, and protection from straying off the practitioners chosen path. Any form of protection needed can be employed by the white image of Santa Muerte.

White is also the color of peace and happiness, bonding, bringing people closer together and is a good choice when working towards stability in any form. Other uses for the white statue are to bring about good luck, spiritual blessings, counseling and guidance, loyalty of a person, purity, and for anything else that the other colors do not cover.

LA ROJA - RED IMAGE

Representations in RED are commonly used to represent love and passion. This color is also used in heating things up in a relationship, passion, excitement, commitment, and marriage. It's used to bring stability in a relationship.

The red Santa Muerte is the one for heating things up, both romantically or passionately. This is often favored by women in love spells. Some men employ her red image to encourage sexual activity or to encounter sexual partners.

Another use for the red image is ensuring fidelity of a partner, to keep someone thinking about you, and to make a person go crazy with love for you. It can be used to calm a rocky relationship and to overcome problems within the home.

LA NEGRA - BLACK IMAGE

Representations in BLACK are commonly used for protection purposes. This includes protection from enemies, protection from evil, protection from witchcraft, hexes, curses, spellwork, and rituals against you. This protection can be used to protect a person, home, business, object, or a piece of property. It can protect a single person, a group of people, or everyone who lives in the same household. Anything that needs protection is best suited to the black image.

The black Santa Muerte is also employed for overcoming problems, and worries. This is the color to select if a person is having problems on the job, whether it is an overwhelming boss or an irritating co-worker. Black is also employed is you know or feel that there is an obstacle in your path keeping you from making progress but you are unable to find the cause or reason for the blockage.

Black Santa Muerte can also be used to combat negativity around you and to overcome spiritual or psychic attacks. And is highly employed to reverse and return spellwork to those who direct it to you.

In matters of healing spiritual illness the black Santa Muerte is invaluable. She can be employed to heal the evil eye, susto (soul loss), and other illnesses that stem from a spiritual nature.

OTHER COLORS USED

NATURAL IMAGE

Representations in NATURAL OR BONE COLOR are

commonly used for bringing peace and harmony. This color can be employed for success in any matter. The natural or bone Santa Muerte is used the same as the white image.

GREEN IMAGE

Representations in GREEN are commonly used for matters of bringing justice to a situation. It's also employed for legal matters, court hearings, legal disputes, law enforcement, and winning the favor of a jury or judge. This is the color to employ to give your attorney the upper hand.

The green Santa Muerte is also used for good luck and money favors. This can include increasing the sales of a business, improving a persons financial situation, selling a home or a piece of property, gambling luck, luck in finding whatever it is that a person is looking for at a reasonable price, pay raises, promotions, or just having extra spending money.

GOLD IMAGE

Representations in GOLD are commonly used for money, prosperity, and success. The gold Santa Muerte is also good for gaining spiritual blessings and asking for special favors.

Special favors which relate to the gold color can include personal success, reaching goals and deadlines, overcoming bad habits, self improvement, motivation, courage, to strengthen a particular talent, to gain new insight of a matter, overcoming fear, and gaining new and fresh ideas.

The gold Santa Muerte can also be employed for success in landing a new job or blessing the opening of a new business.

PURPLE IMAGE

Representations in PURPLE are commonly used for

health related matters. This can include anything related to a person's health whether it's a matter of mental health, physical health, emotional health, or spiritual health.

The purple Santa Muerte can also be employed to increase a person's psychic abilities, to strengthen abilities, or to being out latent abilities. This is the color to use when you want a better or clearer understanding of a card reading or better insight into another form of divination.

You can use this color to ask Santa Muerte for guidance in any form of divination.

BLUE IMAGE

Representations in BLUE are commonly used for wisdom and study. The blue Santa Muerte can be employed for all matters of education, study, and learning. This can include studying for an exam, luck in passing a test, retaining the information learned, strengthening a persons memory level, or remembering names, dates, times, and other information.

I know a school teacher who uses the blue image for controlling her students, to keep them from getting restless during exam time, and to help them better retain the information taught in her class.

The blue Santa Muerte image can also be employed to overcome fear of public speaking or to help a person get their point across to another. It can give the knowledge of words and how to be a better and powerful speaking.

BROWN IMAGE

Representations in BROWN are commonly used for calling and invoking the presence of Santa Muerte. This is used when a person wants her full attention or to offer her guidance in a more visible manner.

The Brown Santa Muerte can also be employed to assist a person in making contact with other spirits with the help of Santa Muerte. This color can aide in all forms of spirit communication and is highly recommended when the spellworker wants to manipulate the spirit or soul of another person.

RAINBOW IMAGE

Representations in RAINBOW, also called THE SEVEN POWERS, are commonly used for all matters. Each of the colors have a special meaning and used for a particular outcome. Although the rainbow image has particular uses for each of the colors, the colors listed above can be applied to the color of the rainbow image.

The GOLD is used for abundance, wealth, and family matters

The PURPLE is used for change for the better, health, and letting go The SILVER is used for good luck, stability, and blessings

The RED is used for passion, love, romance

The COPPER is used for removing negative energies, cleansing, and protection The BLUE is used for spirituality, study, and prosperity

The GREEN is used for money, justice, and success

THE TOOLS OF SANTA MUERTE

You'll notice that not all Santa Muerte statues and picture images are the same. Some may show Santa Muerte holding different items in her hands or include different objects at her feet. The most common image is of Santa Muerte carrying a scythe and a globe. Each of the objects contains a specific significance. Once you begin working with Santa Muerte in the form of a statue, you'll begin to notice that it suddenly looks life-like. The hollow eyes may seem to follow you around the room or the statue may take on a sort of glowing appearance. Energy is strongly felt around the area the image is placed, a sort of electrical current or heat. Her presence lingers. Everyone will have their own experience with her image. Let's explore the parts found on her images for a better understanding of Santa Muerte. I feel the more you know about the spirit or force you are interested in working with the better your experience.

THE SCALES

The scales symbolize justice and judgment. It's believed that when a person's time is over Santa Muerte will be there to greet him or her. She will be carrying her scale which is used to weigh a person deeds. This spiritual judgment is believed to determine is a person goes to heaven or hell. The more good deeds the person has acted on in life, the soul will rise. The more bad deeds the person has acted on, the soul will descend. This belief goes back to ancient Egyptian times and Ma'at, the Goddess of truth, justice, and balance. The dead person's heart was placed on a scale. Ma'at would then balance it. If bad deeds outweighed, the person's heart was devoured by a demon. If good deeds outweighed, then the person's soul was allowed to go on to the afterlife.

Because Santa Muerte is often shown holding the scales of justice she is often associated with Saint Michael. Especially the Santa Muerte images with wings and holding the scales of justice. Although I don't agree with this association, Saint Michael and the Angel of death are two different angels. In my opinion, I believe that the scales are also symbolic of her acceptance to work with a person. The acceptance tips the scale to the right, while rejection tips the scales to the left. This belief stems from a very vivid dream of Santa Muerte after doing an extensive ritual with her which came about because of a student who was eager to begin working with her. In the dream I asked "give me a sign that shows you accepting a person". The scales appeared showing a man sitting on the right side of the scale.

THE SCYTHE

The scythe or sickle (images can be purchased with both. Each has the same meaning) has several meanings; first it is symbolic of endings. This doesn't necessarily meaning the ending of a lifespan as some people relate to it, although in certain conditions it is a symbol of death itself. It can also mean the ending of a time period, a cause, a routine, a dispute, an adventure, a relationship, etc... Endings come in many forms. Santa Muerte uses her scythe to cut away a persons link to something. Santa Muerte's scythe is also symbolic of death since its believed by her followers that when a persons time is up she is the one who comes to escort the soul into the next existence. In this instance her scythe cuts the remaining ties to our worldly life.

The scythe is also a symbol of harvest, prosperity, and hope. It can be said that the scythe she holds is a symbol of harvesting our dreams and desires. A sign of a persons request made to her will flourish, grow, and manifest. It cuts away obstacles that hold a person from making progress and clears a path for guidance. In addition, the scythe can symbolize power and strength. This can be in many forms. It can symbolize the power and strength that Santa Muerte herself carries over all humans and over her realm of the dead. It can also indicate power and strength in a person's spellwork with Santa Muerte, or power and strength over enemies.

THE GLOBE

The globe or the world indicates Santa Muerte's power over the entire world. She is not held back or limited to whom she can rule. She will eventually claim everyone living on earth. Santa Muerte is not limited to location or held back by time or space. She can claim judgment at any given moment. There are no boundaries. It's believed that after God, death (Santa Muerte) is the most powerful figure in the world, since without death there is no life, there is no existence. The globe is an indication that Santa Muerte rules over all race, religion, culture, and belief.....she's just known by other names....but most, if not all, religions have a ruler over death. Here, we call her Santa Muerte.

THE OWL

Sometimes Santa Muerte's statues and picture images include an owl. The owl is symbolic of darkness, nighttime, and keen vision. Santa Muerte's owl companion indicates powerful guidance for those who ask. Many people take their problems and questions to Santa Muerte because they seek the knowledge and a solution....an answer to their blindness. Blindness because they "see" no solution. The owl's sharp vision offers the light a person needs to overcome blindness. It guides a person to solution and success. The owl is also connected to great wisdom and intelligence, hence the term "that wise old owl".

Santa Muerte's owl companion is her messenger. Oftentimes a person who works with Santa Muerte will have visions of an owl through dreams. These dreams are commonly discovered to contain important messages Santa Muerte wishes to share with one of her followers. Owls have also been seen during waking hours as well or the hoot of an owl, although it is not visible, can be heard.

THE HOURGLASS

Santa Muerte's hourglass, or sandglass, symbolizes the hands of time. Each grain of sand is a moment of time itself. Each grain that her hourglass contains is indication of a person's lifespan. When the hourglass is empty, life on earth is over. At the same time death is a continuation of life. This continuation can be in another realm or again here on earth. Some people believe that when a person gets a calling from Santa Muerte each gain of sand in their hourglass are actually tiny microscopic skull and pieces of bone. The hourglass also symbolizes patience. Ask and wait. People who ritually work with Santa Muerte first must give before receiving her gifts. Giving comes in the form of the altar, candles, prayer, and offerings. Once these are made the person waits for her to answer. Patience pays off.

Santa Muerte's hourglass is also connected to time travel. Past, present, and future. She can teach divination to those who she feels are deserving of the knowledge. She can answer questions presented to her concerning a person's life or the history of a place. Any oracle can be dedicated to her in order to receive her guidance in how to most beneficially use it.

THE LAMP

Santa Muerte lamp can be seen as a reflection of her...her presence, her help, her existence, her guidance. With her lamp she lights the path of those who follow her and those who work with her. It lights up a person's direction and/or mental capacity, giving the person a more expanded train of thought. New ideas, new insights, and deeper levels of clarity.

HER ATTIRE

Most commonly Santa Muerte wears a long hooded cloak which extends to her feet, much like the one the

Virgin of Guadalupe wears. It drapes over her boney frame covering almost all of her with the exception of her face, hands, feet, and sometimes the lower half of her legs. Her cloak is symbolic of the protection she extends to her devotees. She opens her cloak wide and covers the person with it to keep them safe from whatever it is they need protection from.

A person can have just one single white statue of Santa Muerte and change the color of her cloak according to the work being done. The basic colors for cloaks are red, white, and black but other colors can be made as well. There are several places that sell cloaks or robes already made for Santa Muerte but these are usually very expensive. If you are handy with a sewing machine they can be made very inexpensively at home. Some women make her a wedding gown which is draped over the statue when ritually working with her for marriage and commitment purposes.

Other colors that may serve well are blue, purple, gold, and brown. Easily dress her in different robes. This keeps from having to purchase different color statues for related spellwork.

WORKING WITH SANTA MUERTE

OFFERINGS MADE TO SANTA MUERTE

Offerings to Santa Muerte should be gifts that come form the heart, not items that are used to simply decorate her altar. These offerings are extensions of yourself. They are extensions of your faith and loyalty. In this section of the course we will talk about offerings given to Santa Muerte. These are things that are appropriate for her and items that she is known to be fond of.

You can choose any of these offerings as you feel you are drawn to give. You can even offer a combination of these offerings.

I would suggest that you try to keep food offerings down to a minimum, except for bread offerings. Other food offerings are best given only once a week. Keep in mind that I am talking about food offerings placed on the altar that is not part of a spellwork with Santa Muerte.

WATER

At least one clear glass of water should be kept on the altar at all times. The glass should be clear with no designs. Plastic containers should never be used. Tap water is fine to use but if you are in an area with hard water cleaning the glass could be difficult. Using filtered water will help to alleviate the gunk that sticks to the glass. Water glasses should be cleaned and replaced with fresh water once a week. If you notice the water becomes cloudy or grey dispose of the water outdoors and replace with fresh water. This is a sign of negativity around you which was captured in the glass.

INCENSE

Santa Muerte is fond of copal, cedar, myrrh, patchouli, and nag champa for general burning. Stick, cone, and loose incense is acceptable. Otherwise here is a list of some incense and what they can be used for on her altar.

Rose incense can be offered for love, passion, sexual matters, and lust.

Sandalwood can be used for blessings and prosperity.

Copal can be used for purification and success.

Myrrh can be used for protection.

Jasmine can be used for money and good luck.

Musk can be used for healing.

Carnation can be used for love related matters.

TOBACCO

Tobacco in the form of cigarettes or cigars can be used as offerings to Santa Muerte. I like to leave an ashtray, wooden matches, and a pack of cigarettes on her altar for her to indulge in any time she wishes. These can be lit and the smoke blown over her image as an offering and for purification purposes. If you are a non-smoker you can just wave the cigarette around and allow the smoke to make contact or once it's lit leave it to burn in the ashtray. The tobacco can also be used for invoking her.

BREAD

Bread offerings are very much enjoyed by Santa Muerte. Any type of bread is appropriate. Through my own experience I have noticed quicker responses when I designate a day for a certain type of bread. I give bread offerings two days out of the week. On Tuesdays I like to offer brown, wheat, or rye bread and on Thursdays I offer Santa Muerte white bread, including white wheat.

Bread offerings can be placed on a plate or a clay terracotta tray and placed on her altar. It should be changed when the bread gets hard. Don't allow it to stay long enough to get moldy though. Usually a piece of bread will be good for at least four or five days before it needs to be removed.

Making a routine of offering bread to the Santa Muerte ensures that everyone in the household will always have enough to eat. It keeps hunger away from the home and encourages plenty of good nutritious foods we have in the home and enough to share if need be.

Some good choices of bread offerings are slices of French bread, white bread, pumpernickel, wheat, rye, whole grain, pita, and also tortillas. Once a bread offering given to Santa Muerte is removed from the altar it should be bagged up and scattered outdoors for the wild animals and birds to feed on.

FRUIT

Fruit offerings given to Santa Muerte should be good quality fresh fruits. Do not place fruit on the altar if the outside skin is marred in any way. The best selections are those with a fragrant odor and the outside skin is smooth and free of surface blemishes, nicks, dings, wormholes, or breakage.

APPLES

I have found through working with her that sweet red apples are favored over sour green apples.

My own personal favorites are the red delicious apples and the gala apples. In my opinion these two types of apples are the sweetest and most of the grocery stores always have them in abundance no matter what time of year it is. If you want to use green apples, save them to use as part of a ritual or spellwork nut offer the sweet red ones when you are giving an offering from the heart.

Apples are good energies of love and luck. As the fruit begins to look a little old or begins to wilt and change colors this is when they should be removed from the altar. Again, bag them up and throw them outdoors for the wild to feed on.

ORANGES

Oranges on the altar are symbolic of health and harmony and carry a good supply of these energies. The best oranges I have found for altar use are the regular navel oranges and valencia oranges. In my opinion these are the sweetest and both last a long time on the altar without rotting too quickly.

I also use the blood oranges but tend to use them more for spellwork and dedication purposes. In dedication use the blood orange is by far the best. These can be used when dedicating an object to Santa Muerte such as divination tools or when you are dedicating yourself to working with her. Since the blood orange, not only for its name but also its red color symbolizes blood itself.

COCONUT

Coconut can be used on the altar but it should first be broken open and the milk drained into a small cup. Both the meat of the coconut and the milk are offered at the same time. I like to dress the feet of her statue with just a little of the coconut milk. I really think she enjoys the coconut bath...lol. The coconut meat will last several days on the altar but the milk will stale quickly so remove the milk after a day or two. If you remove the meat from the shell it makes a good offering dish later. Coconuts carry a lot of cleansing and grounding energy.

BANANA

Bananas should be removed from the altar after 24 hours since they rot very quickly. Also bananas have a tendency to attract small flies and they attract other insects as well. You don't want insects or flies swarming around her altar. Bananas are great sources of fertility and fidelity energies.

MELONS

Watermelon is another fruit that should be removed after 24 hours for the same reason as oranges. Other good choices of melon for the Santa Muerte altar include cantaloupe, and honeydew. Melons on the altar attract prosperity.

PINEAPPLE

Pineapples can be placed on the altar either sliced or whole. If they are removed before rotting takes hold you can cut the rinds and place them in your bathwater to bring the blessings of Santa Muerte to you. Pineapple on the altar is good for general protection purposes.

OTHER FRUITS

Other types of fruit that make good offerings to Santa Muerte include mango, grapes, pears, plums, strawberries, peaches, apricot, blackberry, blueberry, cherry, cranberry, figs, grapefruit, kiwi, lemon, lime, nectarine, papaya, persimmon, and pomegranate. With this list you will always be able to find fresh fruit that's in season.

FLOWERS

Try to always keep a fresh vase of flowers on the Santa Muerte altar. Any flower may be given as an offering. You can also place specific types of flowers on the altar according to the work you are doing or the energies you want around you. When the plant material begin to wilt or turn brown, snip the rotting portions off with a pair of scissors and remove it from the altar.

Red flowers are symbolic of love and heart felt matters.

White flowers are symbolic of purity, cleansing, and blessing.

Yellow or gold flowers are symbolic of wealth.

Pink flowers are symbolic of kindness and friendship.

OTHER PLANT MATERIAL

Other plants and herbs Santa Muerte favors are aloe vera, acacia, agave, agueweed, asafetida, ash, basil, balm of gilead, balmony, bamboo, banyan, belladonna, benzoin, betel nut, bladderwrack, boldo, boxwood, buckeye nuts, camphor, cayenne, celandine, chaparral, chicory, china berry, cumin, devil pod, devil's claw, devils shoestring, dragon's blood, fava beans, ironweed, knotweed, licorice root, mastic, milk thistle, money pods, oregano, pecan, poplar, poppy seed, rosemary, rue, rosemary, star anise, spearmint, stinging nettle, false unicorn root, vanilla, verbena, witches grass and yucca.

BEVERAGES

Good choices of beverages include coffee, red, white, or pink wine, brandy, tequila, rum, beer, sherry, whiskey, tea, hot chocolate, licorice liquor, and wine coolers. These should be removed within 48 hours after the offering has been made. Make sure to always serve beverages in glass, never plastic. Santa Muerte has a taste for hard liquor...lol...I have left small shot glasses of whiskey for her and the next day the glass was completely empty. I have to jokingly tell her

"Santa slow down!"...lol

OTHER SUITABLE OFFERINGS

Holy Water, avocados, Tabasco sauce, honey, magnets, soil from different locations, toys, money, siete machos cologne, hard candy, chocolate squares, mints, Rosaries, jewelry, medals, milagros, sugar skulls, cakes and other baked goods, photos, letters, written prayers, and feather boas.

CONSTRUCTION OF THE SANTA MUERTE ALTAR

Most people who work with Santa Muerte have a place dedicated in their homes for her altar. The Santa Muerte altar gives the person a special place to do spellwork and rituals. It also gives the person a place where he or she can go to connect with Santa Muerte and to spend quality time with her. This is Santa Muerte's special place to rest in the person's home. When you create an altar for Santa Muerte it becomes a point of focus when you want to make contact with her. It becomes a place of empowerment, intuition, and the person a way for easier connection, clearer messages, and closer links.

Using the Santa Muerte altar regularly will be a starting point for the person to begin establishing and building a strong working relationship with her. By continuously using this area it will start to build positive energy in and around that space. Any place spiritual work is done energy builds there. The more it's used the more energy that collects. For this reason it's important to choose a special place for communication and connection. This buildup of spiritual energy grows each time the space is used for spiritual work. The more spiritual energy that a space contains the easier it is for the person to communicate. The closer the person comes to Santa Muerte. A person will even find that their concentration levels are deeper more focused, with fewer distractions. Many people even find that fresh flowers seem to last longer when placed on her altar than in any other place in the home.

If the person uses their Santa Muerte altar on a regular basis their relationship with her will be thousands of times more gratifying. Her altar can literally transform the life of her devotee. A person can use the Santa Muerte altar any time they want to make contact with her, anytime they want her counsel and guidance. Her altar can be used for healing, prayer, communication, meditation, guidance, protection, self-development, advice, spellwork, and just to feel her presence. After the altar has been used for a while both the quality and quantity of energy will increase.

The altar may even begin to give a person the feeling of peace and calmness whenever they are near it. Some people claim that they feel a rush of energy emitting from the altar. Others have reported feeling comfortable temperature changes or tingling over their body or that they instantly receive mental images or see streaks of colored light as they approach the altar. It becomes a sacred space where the person is more receptive to hearing her messages.

People who have erected Santa Muerte altars in their home claim that family members get along better, there is more communication between them, more patience and understanding, more sharing and giving, more peaceful family time, less arguments, less stress, less tears, less frustration, and more happier moments. Things just seem to run smoothly in the household.

The more a person works with Santa Muerte at her altar the more comfortable they become, the more knowledgeable and receptive they become. It personalizes their connection to Santa Muerte. The person may find him/herself going to the altar when they are faced with making an important decision or when they feel confused about a situation.

The Santa Muerte altar doesn't have to be anything elaborate. It can be as small or as large as the person wants it to be. It can be set up on a shelf or on a small table in a corner of the room. I have found that old dressers make great altars since they have drawers that can be used to store things inside such as incense, candles, candle snuffers, matches, prayers, or different altar cloths.

Any kind of surface can be used (although I tend to try and stay away from plastic in all my spiritual work as much as possible) but I suggest if you are going to purchase a table to use as an altar, first try looking at used furniture stores, thrift stores, and garage sales. You'd be amazed at what kind of treasures you can find there and at a fraction of the cost of something new. If you look around you'll come up with all kinds of surfaces you could use. I have seen some altars made from cardboard boxes, turned upside down and a nice cloth thrown over the top! Be creative, let your imagination flow and your intuition be your guide.

The most important thing in consideration to the altar is its location. It should be in a place that is comfortable and where the person will get the most privacy. Wherever it is placed make sure that there are no curtains or any other flammable items near which could pose a fire hazard when incense and candles are lit. Once a location is selected and the surface erected the next thing that must be done is a thorough spiritual cleansing.

There are many methods of cleansing altars but the easiest is by spiritual fumigation (smudging).
To cleanse the Santa Muerte altar you are going to clear it of both surface dirt and of negative energies, the "spiritual dirt".

Begin by wiping down the entire altar surface. Make sure to wipe down underneath, around, back and top of it. I wouldn't suggest cleaning it with chemical cleansers; instead use plain tap water, Holy Water, or an herbal spiritual "tea". Some herbs that are good to make into a liquid and used for cleaning would be sage, rosemary, and rue. These herbs are known to clear away negative energies as well as provide a good liquid for removing surface dirt.

To make an herbal tea used for cleaning, not drinking, bring

4 cups of water to a boil. Remove from heat and add ½ cup of the dry or fresh herb to the water. Cover and let simmer for 30 minutes or until the liquid is cool. Strain out the herb and save the liquid. Use the reserved liquid as a cleaner by dipping a cloth into the solution.

Once you are finished cleaning off the surface dirt you will need to clear it from negative energy that has gathered on it. There are many ways you can clear negative energy from an item but here I'll tell you how to do it by what is called "smudging".

To smudge an item for the purpose of removing built up negativity you can use dry herb or incense. If you want to use dry herb you can use sage and if you want to use incense you can use either myrrh, or frankincense. Both methods do the same thing. With dry herb you will need to have a heatproof container or a censor and a charcoal disk to burn the herb. Either way, all you have to do is allow the smoke from the incense or the herb to come in contact with all the parts of the altar. The sacred smoke removes negative energy by itself. Just make sure the smoke touches every part of the altar.

Once it's cleaned of surface dirt and cleared of negative energy you can begin placing items on the altar, this is the fun part. Cover the top of the altar with a nice fabric. Choose colors that are pleasing to the eye. in my opinion a simple white cloth is best. I have several altar cloths in different colors. I'll change them out according to the work being done. Loud colors and wild prints tend to be too distracting. I tend to burn a lot of candles on my altar so to protect my altar fabric I purchased an inexpressive clear plastic shower curtain liner, cut it to the size of my altar and lay the plastic over the top of the fabric. This way if any of the melted wax happens to drip the fabric will be safe from stains.

TO BAPTIZE A SANTISIMA MUERTE STATUE

The most important part of devotion to Santa Muerte is Her statue, which gives her a body, a physical object through which Her presence and power can manifest. The more you work with Her at Her altar, the more power the objects on Her altar become. This is especially true for the statue(s) placed upon it.

Whenever you purchase or make a new statue of Santa Muerte, it is important to baptize it and dedicate it to Her. If you're lucky enough to find a priest or deacon to bless the statue, that is highly recommended; however, since it's extremely unlikely you will find such a member of the clergy to do so, you can bless and baptize Her statues yourself.

To do this, first clean the statue of any dust or dirt, and then pass it through some incense smoke (white copal being the best, or some Santa Muerte incense that usually contains copal). Then, take a bowl of holy water, which can be obtained at any Catholic Church, and add a few drops of Siete Machos cologne or some Florida Water.

Begin with the basic devotional prayers, and ask God for permission to invoke the Most Holy Death. Lean the statue backwards over the bowl of water, and cup your hand in the bowl, pouring water over the forehead of the statue three times, saying: "I baptize You (first handful) in the name of the Father, (second handful) and of the Son, (third handful) and of the Holy Spirit. Amen."

Alternately, you can hold a bottle of holy water and asperge the statue three times with it as you say the words of baptism.

If you have a rosary of the appropriate color for the statue, you may also dip it in the bowl of water and then wrap it around the statue.

Now bless the statue with cigar smoke. Traditionally this is done by "shotgunning" the cigar, where you light the end of it, and then turn it around and place the lit end in your mouth and, closing your lips around it blow smoke out all over the statue. Shotgunning creates a lot of sacred tobacco smoke mixed with your own breath, but as some people find this difficult, you may also simply put the unlit end in your mouth and blow the smoke that way.

After blessing the statue all over with the smoke, talk to Santa Muerte and ask Her to come into the statue to receive devotion from you. Finally, place the newly baptized statue on Her altar: it is now cleansed and consecrated for your devotional and spiritual work.

I would also recommend following this with prayers such as the Litany and/or Rosary, but any devotional prayers from your heart would be appropriate at this point

ADDING ALTAR ITEMS

First if you have a statue of Santa Muerte or a special photograph you are going to be working with this should take center stage. This is the item that goes directly in the center of the altar.

Secondly, the Santa Muerte altar should have an aloe plant hanging upside down from the back wall. The aloe plant, roots and all, should be tied with a red string or red ribbon and just allowed to hang freely. The aloe is one of her most prized plants. You can even have another small potted aloe vera plant growing in a clay pot on her altar. The aloe can be placed anywhere on the altar. The one hanging from the wall should be located somewhere close to her head.

To keep a good supply of money coming into your home there should be a clay or crystal vase to the right of her image. Seven coins are placed in the vase, these represent the seven days of the week, and seven single stemmed yellow or gold flowers of any kind are placed inside the vase. Also include a small magnet. The vase is then filled with Holy Water and changed weekly. If you are not interested in keeping a good supply of money coming in to your home than the vase of flowers can be placed anywhere on the altar and the coins can be omitted.

A Rosary is always a nice addition to the altar. This is normally just hung from her extended hand or you can also just place it at her feet on the altar. Personally I like hanging it from her hands. This is the traditional way.

Any plants that you have growing on the altar should be watered with Holy Water only. Keep in mind, just because Santa Muerte is the saint of death doesn't mean she doesn't like Holy Water around her. lol. In Mexico Santa Muerte is a blend of everything, including Christianity.

It's common to see Saint statues who share Santa Muerte's altar. Some believe that Santa Muerte is jealous of who she shares her space with. This is true to some extent and there are few Saints who she will except on her own personal space. Santa Muerte will become jealous with others who share her space too, not just Saints. Over the years the only ones I have found that she will accept on her altar are the Virgin of Guadalupe, St Lazarus, and Jesus. She seems to also accept small statues or images of the two Aztec gods Mictlantecuhtli and his wife Mictecacihuatl. If any others are placed on her altar she will not work for you. She has also been known to throw a temper tantrum by causing bad luck until they are removed. Even for the other images that she will allow to share her space Santa Muerte demands to take the center stage. What I mean by this is Santa Muerte should stand higher on the altar than any others who share her space. It's a good idea to elevate her statue so that it is taller than any others. She wants to be the focal point and show everyone that this is her space.

A bible or a special book of prayers of your choice should be kept on the left side of the altar, towards the back. This is used to randomly open the book and read the prayers to her. She loves hearing a devotee reciting prayers for her. You can of course read the prayers of your choosing but I feel it adds more depth to the time spent at the altar if you allow her to select the prayers she wants to hear instead. If you randomly flip through the pages she will stop you on the ones she wants to hear.

The bible or book of prayers is kept to the back left of the altar because in nature the left side is related to study, contemplation, and reflection. The right side is a reflection of strength and
power. So this is the side (the right side) where you want ongoing energies to come in....such as the vase of coins to

attract a good supply of money towards you.

The center back of the altar is for camouflage, hiding, and secrecy. This is where you want to keep things that you want to keep hidden from others such as secrets, or if you are acting as a false friend. What I mean by this is sometimes in spellwork we want our friends close but our enemies closer. There may be times when you may want to be around a person, not because you like them, but because you need to watch them. The rear center of the altar would be where you would write the name of the person, maybe tape his or her eyes shut, and placed in the back to keep them from knowing your secret.

The center front of the Santa Muerte altar is a powerhouse. This is where you may want to perform spellwork as opposed to one side or the other. This is the place that you will use for the greatest effect of all. Right at the base of Santa Muerte's feet is where we give the greatest honor to her.

Candles can be placed anywhere you feel fit. Unless the candles are part of a ritual working. In that case you would want to place it in front of her, again at her feet for the greatest effect. If you have ever noticed in documentaries and old films, even in old books when a person goes before a king or queen....any person of royalty......they are always shown at the front and center.
This is because it's the position of respect and honor.

WORKING WITH SANTA MUERTE

There are many misconceptions when it comes to working with Santa Muerte, at least in my opinion. I have known people who have worked with her for most of their lives and never experienced any of the things people talk about. Through my own experience with her I have never known her to be vindictive or hateful. Granted, Santa Muerte is a very jealous force to work with and she is very stingy when it comes to her own personal space (her altar) but don't we all have something that we consider to be "off limits" to everyone else? Most of my female friends and family members feel this way about their purses.....off limits! Most men I know feel this way about their wallets. Our spiritual altars are usually "off limits" to others. I don't think this is such a bad thing.

I have heard some people talk about how working with Santa Muerte is a form of devil worship.
Again, I completely disagree with this belief. Santa Muerte is a blend of Mesoamerican and Catholic beliefs. Many of her followers are Catholic. Rituals or rites dedicated to Santa Muerte are very closely linked to Christian rites. Many of her most popular prayers have a Christian feel to them and many who work with her also pray to God and Saints. In my opinion, I feel that this misconception of Santa Muerte being devil worship comes from her appearance. Skeletons, skulls, and bones frighten many people. I feel that this misconception also comes from the connection of Santa Muerte to death. I'm guessing that it has something to do with the way a person views death itself. If they are frightened of death than obviously they will fear Santa Muerte. Maybe it comes from how a person views God and the devil. God being life, and the devil being death. Who knows, but these are ideas that have popped into my head. There are a couple of Christian Saints who are associated with bones as well. We have San Pascual, Saint Denis who is headless and holds his own head in his right hand. We

33

also have St Jerome who is mostly pictured with a skull.

Santa Muerte does not separate good and evil. There is no distinction between the two in her eyes. It's worth mentioning again that the distinction between good or evil workings is in the eye of the spellworker or petitioner. No person is ever forced to work the darker side of the art.

Santa Muerte can be called on for anything. No problem is too big and no problem is too small.
One isn't more important over another. She can be called on to bring back a lost love, to get someone out of jail or confinement, to bring love and marriage, protection from all dangers and enemies, protection from evil spirits, to cure all illnesses and health problems, to get revenge on someone, for guidance, for knowledge, to increase your income, for good luck, for gambling luck, to do good or evil.....you name it she will do it. Santa Muerte is a complete and total magical system in herself. This is very hard to come by. Most gods, goddesses, saints, and deities have certain areas they are called for. Santa Muerte is complete.

The first thing that should be done before calling on Santa Muerte for help is to give her a gift of yourself. Make something personal. Its well worth the effort and time it takes if you take a little while to make a gift for her with your own two hands. This should actually be done at the very beginning before your fist work with her, before your first request, and before your fist candle and prayer. But if you have already started work with Santa Muerte you can still make something. Better late than never, right. I can't express how much this will help in your future relationship with her. Making a gift for her with your own two hands serves not only as a very special and personal offering to her but also shows your faith and willingness to work with her.
It also shows her that you are not all about taking or calling on her only when something is needed. A handmade gift is

always something very special.

Santa Muerte's feast day falls on all souls day, although some people celebrate it on August 15.
The day of the dead is her special day of the year. I have not found an official day of the week which is dedicated to Santa Muerte but with the help of friends who have been working with her for years and through my own experience Wednesday seems to be the day where more requests are granted. More spellwork I have started on this day seems to always have a good outcome so I take that as a most valuable sign from Santa Muerte herself.

I have heard a few people say that her altar should always have a candle burning on it. Not that I disagree with this belief, I have just never found the lack of candle light to interfere with the work being performed or the lack of attention she gives to someone who only offers candle light once a week. I'll usually burn a small votive on her altar every Wednesday (her day) and a large seven day glass encased candle for her at the beginning of each month. These are not candles that relate to spellwork or requests; these are lights that I give to her out of faith and devotion.

I mentioned how one should place a vase on her altar with a magnet, flowers and coins in order to keep a good supply of money coming it to the household. Well there is another traditional version of this special vase. A clay vase can be placed anywhere on the altar filled with fresh tap water. Six coins are dropped into the vase and six white flowers of any kind are placed inside. The flowers can be any type of flower but they must be white. The six flowers are for the six good spirits that protect you from the six devils (sprits of darkness) who can harm you on six successive days of the week. A seventh white flower is set directly on the altar next to the vase, not in water. This seventh flower is left out of the water which is symbolic that you believe Santa Muerte is the seventh spirit who protects you on the day that is left open by the other six protective angels. Confusing I know but keep reading that last sentence and it will soon begin to make sense...lol....Santa Muerte fills in the seventh day of the week.

Traditionally this vase containing the six coins and the six white flowers is used when making a request or when doing spellwork with Santa Muerte. After Santa Muerte has granted a request you would take the six white flowers and the six coins in the vase with water and leave them on the threshold of the cemetery. Take the entire vase; don't take the stuff out of it. You can also leave them on the first grave you see as you go inside the entrance of the cemetery. Then you would just turn and walk away. On your way home you should then stop by the store and pick up four white votive candles, four red ones, and four black ones. When you get home these candles are placed around the Santa Muerte statue or photograph neatly arranged in a circle.
And offer all these candles to her all at once for helping you. This will keep her happy and eager to help when you call on her.

Another way to pay respect to her or to thank her for answering a request is once the request is granted make her a huge buffet of different flavorful foods and sweet treats. These can be placed on plates and glasses and set out on her altar for her to feast. I have found this very pleasing to her since she likes to indulge. Santa Muerte doesn't actually eat the food offered to her, not in the same way we consume food. Santa Muerte, actually all spirits that food is given to, consumes the "energy" of the food. This is why the food rots so quickly. When the energy of the food is gone the food rots.

When making a request to Santa Muerte always be serious. Make sure that you know exactly what you want, when you want it, and how you want it done before presenting it to her. Don't go before the Santa Muerte unprepared. She is a serious force to work with and doesn't take kindly to laziness, disarray, or confusion. Have everything prepared and ready beforehand even if you have to go over it several times. She won't take vengeance on this kind of disorganization but she won't help you either. It's okay for her to be lazy but it is never okay for you to be.

Another thing Santa Muerte really likes is to have her statues washed often. I usually add some Siete Machos cologne to a bowl of Holy Water and sponge down her images with the mixture. For those who are working with a photograph of Santa Muerte as opposed to a statue you can wash the frame of the picture for the same effect. Try not to saturate the statue or frame with the liquid. Instead just lightly dampen the image with the liquid. This isn't a bath; it's more of a freshener. Something to freshen her up a bit. At the same time it keeps the image free of physical dust and debris.

Other water additives that can be used that have proven to be good are patchouli, floral water, flordia water, rue water, witch hazel, gardenia, rose, eucalyptus, cypress, frankincense, myrrh, and peppermint oils.

Any candle placed on her altar should be brand new and clean. Don't use dusty candles. The only candles that can be relit for Santa Muerte are those that were used for devotional purposes, those that are lit specially in her honor as opposed to those used in spellwork. Purple is a good color candle to burn for her as devotionals. You can also burn white ones in her honor. Otherwise candles are burnt for their related purposes. The brighter the color of the candle used on the Santa Muerte altar the better.

When lighting candles for Santa Muerte don't allow your mind to wander in negative directions. In every single magical art known faith plays an important part of the work. From the beginning when you first take a request before her until the end stay in a positive frame of mind and perform the work without hesitation. Words spoken, prayers, and requests should be made in a strong and powerful tone. This is not the time to show a timid side. Don't approach Santa Muerte in a forceful manner but do approach her in a strong, positive manner.

Your hands should be washed before handling any of the candles presented to her. Getting in the routine of hand washing before performing spellwork with Santa Muerte is good habit since it keeps you from bringing in outside energies which could be negative in nature.

For those who need a refresher on candle colors following is a list of candle colors and their basic uses.
White = all purpose, purification
Red = love, passion and to heat things up
Black = protection and enemy work
Pink = love, friendship
Purple = health and general offering

Wooden matches are the best to light candles and incense on Santa Muerte's altar. The next best is paper matches, and the least favored is a butane lighter. I don't like using lighters on spiritual altars if it can be avoided because of the energies of the fuel it adds to the atmosphere. Candles and incense offered to Santa Muerte should always be lit with your dominate hand. This is the most powerful since the non-dominate carries weakness. All candles lit on the Santa Muerte altar, no matter what the purpose of the candle is for, should never be blown out with your breath. Either pinch out the flame with your fingers or use a candle snuffer.

Santa Muerte likes fragrant incense, something with a

distinct aroma as opposed to mild and hard to detect scents. Some of the best fragrances I have found for her are rose (but one with a strong odor), patchouli (one of favorites), nag champa, cedar, dragon's blood, and copal (another of her favorites). Incense offerings should be placed on the right side of her statue or picture.

Remember, with Santa Muerte the right side is the direction for reflection, strength, power, and ongoing energies. She's just a little different than working with other forces. You can try the incense in other locations on the altar and experiment with it a bit but I have written this course through my own trials and errors and those of some friends so it may save you some time. But do experiment.

I have found that the number nine seems to connect with Santa Muerte. I haven't figured out what the exact connection is but I have found that by incorporating the number nine into spellwork and requests I get a stronger outcome of the work. The end result seems to last longer and it's felt more strongly. Now I incorporate the number nine into the number of times I recite a prayer to her. Sometimes I'll section her candles into nine equal sections and burn them over a period of nine days. I've tried to also incorporate the number nine into the offerings I place on her altar. I may offer her nine pieces of fruit, a string of beads in groupings of nine or with nine colors, or nine cones of incense in one single day.

If you are one who travels a lot you may want to consider having a portable altar that is easy to travel with. Whenever I travel I like Santa Muerte to travel with me so I'll always take her along. Small portable altars travel well and are easily placed inside a suitcase or a carry bag.

There are many good websites that offer pre-made portable altars which are ready for use as soon as they arrive but they are usually a little costly. You can make these yourself out of things that you probably already have laying around the house for just pennies.

Some ideas for portable altars are old briefcases, roomy wooden boxes that lock shut and have a handle for carrying. I have even seen a small one made out of an old metal lunchbox! These items can be decorated and painted in any way that is pleasing to you (and Santa Muerte). The inside can be lined with felt, velvet, or burlap and decorated with small photos, crosses, milagros, and a small Santa Muerte statue or a photo of Santa Muerte affixed inside. The possibilities are endless.

All prayers offered to the Santa Muerte should be recited in a slow and forceful manner. Never rush through a prayer with her or she will ignore your work and your request. Prayers are best if they are memorized but if this is not the case then reading them is acceptable as long as you sound like your talking to her and not like you're reading word for word on a page. Santa Muerte has always seemed to me a little picky about how she is approached.

In the beginning, its better to only be working on one spell instead of multiple ones. Later as the working relationship becomes closer between you and Santa Muerte more things can be taken on. I have never known her to give multiple blessings to a new devotee at the same time. This is her way of "testing the waters" with new followers. Once she understands your own personal way of working she will eventually give way to work more on the lines of the way you do things and at the speed you work.

Just as the Santa Muerte altar has certain places on the altar witch correspond to different needs there are also two locations which can be used to attract other outside spirits to you or to repel other spirits. Santa Muerte always gives the practitioner the choice. This is on the wall behind her altar either on the left or on the right. On the right side of her statue a small young aloe is tied with a red ribbon and hung upside down on the wall. Here on the right side is for attracting good and helpful spirits to you. On the left side of her statue a small young aloe is tied with a red ribbon and hung upside down on the wall. Here on the left side is for repelling and driving away spirits. This is important to know especially if you are planning on calling the spirit of a person other than Santa Muerte at the Santa Muerte altar. You see this commonly done during love spells when the practitioner calls the spirit of the target person to influence them to surrender to the practitioner's desire.

The aloe vera plant is one of Santa Muerte's most favored plants. When one wants to work spells of love or of domination the aloe can be used as a proxy or witness in order to further and strengthen the spellwork being performed. The aloe vera grows in both male and female forms.
The male aloe vera grows shorter leaves which could grow up to about a foot. The male leaves are bright green and contain a bunch of small white spots. It also grows in clumps. The female aloe vera grows longer and broader leaves. The leaves also seem to be firmer than the male.
The color of the female leaves are green also but with bluish spots. Sometimes the female doesn't produce the small white spots on her leaves. Instead of growing in clumps the female plants tend to grow more in the form of larger rosettes. So what does this have to do with anything?

Being Santa Muerte's most prized plants she places a gender upon them just as they are in nature. To strengthen love spells or domination and controlling spells male plants are used to represent the man you want to control and female plants are used to represent the woman you want to control. To do this all you have to do is take the plant to Santa Muerte at her altar and name it. This is as simple as holding the plant up close to the Santa Muerte Statue and saying "this male plant is now a representation of (mans name)" or vise versa. Then take some red thread and tie it around the roots. Then hang it on Santa Muerte's hands so that the person ceases control over their actions and is under the influence of Santa Muerte and your desires.

This same idea can be used for binding a person. Once the plant is hung on Santa Muerte's hands you would then recite the prayer of the aloe (given later).

DEDICATING THE ALTAR

Once the Santa Muerte altar is set up and spiritually cleansed it should be formally dedicated to her. This is easily accomplished through prayer.

Light a white candle and place it in front of the Santa Muerte image that is the focal point of the altar and recite the following prayer to Santa Muerte.

Santisima Muerte
I humbly kneel before you
Before this space which has
Been created in your name
Here you sit in the throne
of this house
I dedicate this space
To your most powerful presence
And to honor you from
My world on earth
Allow this space to bridge the gap
From me to you
Most powerful Santa Muerte
Please accept this space
As my gift to you
Here you are most welcome
And your visits most appreciated
Allow this space to be free
From outside forces
Who wish to intrude
Keep this space solely
For your energies
Your power
Your presence
Your spirit
Your help
And your blessings
Amen
(Recite three our fathers).

Allow the candle to burn. During the burning of the candle find a few minutes to come back and talk to Santa Muerte from your heart. Do this anytime, but before the candle is completely consumed. Sit before the altar and mentally or verbally call Santa Muerte. Ask her in your own words to fill the space with her energy. Speak to her from your heart just as you would speak to a close friend or family member who was sitting in the room with you. Tell her how eager you are to work with her and to receive her messages and counsel. Always remember to be respectful of her and thank her for her presence.

Now on a blank piece of paper write your name all in capital letters. If you choose, you can use a photo of yourself instead. Fold the paper over only once, making sure to fold it towards you and not away from you. Place this under her statue or under her picture if that's what you are using on the altar. This stays there all the time.

After dedicating the altar you should go on to asking her permission to accept you as a devotee.
The following prayer is one that I normally suggest to those wanting to have a working relationship with her.

Acceptance Prayer
Santa Muerte
Look upon me with kindness
And see that I am sincere
Cast upon me your blessings
Which grant me the confirmation
To call upon your most
Powerful aide and counsel
At this moment
I humbly place my faith
In your power
Be my protector, my hope

Be my light
In times of blindness
Be my counsel
In times of confusion
By my eyes and my ears
In times of unknowing
Be my aide
In times of need
Be the powerful force
Who accepts me as
A humble and devoted
Follower
Amen

PROTECTING BEFORE INVOKING

Even though Santa Muerte protects a person its always good practice in any magical art to make a habit of safeguarding yourself before tapping in to the world of the spirit.

A rule of thumb in human survival and in the magical art is to look after your own wellbeing first. Anything else is a bonus. Taking protective measures is very important. Santa Muerte rules over the dead. With that being said, Santa Muerte is also accompanied by other spirits. All magical arts involve the mysteries of the world, unseen and hidden dangers. It's a deliberate tap into a place outside the world we know....the spirit world. Any pursuit involving the non-physical world warrants special protection. Without protection you leave yourself open for attack. Dangers are not always what they seem.....they come in many forms. You have to always stay one step ahead and continuously cautious. So let me say again that a good rule of thumb in human survival and in the magical art is to look after your own wellbeing first.

Anything else is a bonus.

In this section I'll quickly go over some basic protective measures and end this topic with some prayers which serve well for protection.

Anything you feel is sacred and offers protection can be used to shield yourself from hidden danger. There are also a ton of Saints who have patronage over protection. I'm a firm believer that protection comes in two forms......prayer and a physical object (sacred object)....... Prayers are extremely powerful and should be used in all spiritual work. Since prayer is actually

"unseen" with our eyes at the moment we are praying, our faith in them is needed, strong faith....but at times human nature makes us wonder if our prayers are being heard. Sacred objects add to our natural human need for something "physical", something we can actually

"touch", "feel" and "see"..... so both forms of protection is best.....prayer and something physical. Besides fulfilling our instinct for "the physical", sacred objects are needed for their "ability". Many of these objects have their own natural protective power either by shape, representation, materials they are made from, or by some unexplained mystery.

Protective objects can either be worn around the neck, held in the hand, carried in a pocket, or placed in the area you will be working in. You might also choose to have more than one object of protection (sacred object). Different types of metals have their own unique properties, some more protective than others. By far, out of all the metals, silver offers the widest range of protection. Silver protects from bad energies, witchcraft, enemies, and evil spirits. Anything made from silver would be a good choice.

If you are Catholic or Christian there are several sacramentals (not sacraments, they are different) that offer protection to the wearer. Sacramentals are very powerful.

BLESSED SALT SACRAMENTAL

Blessed salt is an instrument of grace which is used to protect one from evil and demonic influences. Blessed salt may be sprinkled in the area you are working in to protect from being attacked by the unseen. It can also b sprinkled around doorways to protect from hidden enemies.

Sprinkling blessed salt around the perimeter of your property places a protective barrier around your entire home. You can even put a few grains in drinking water to bring astonishing spiritual and physical benefits. Any amount of salt can be taken to the church for the official blessing by a priest or it can be blessed at home.

SACRAMENTAL SAINT MEDALS

Many people wear Saint Medals on chains around their necks. These are also protective sacramentals and more effective when they are blessed. Some of more popular Saint Medals used for protection are St. Michael, St. Benedict Jubilee Medal, St. Cyprian, St. Basil the Great, and St. Margaret of Antioch. The Saint Benedict Jubilee Medal can also be hung over doorways of your home for safety and protection and are often placed in the fields, in the foundations of

buildings or attached to automobiles to call down powerful blessings and the protection of St. Benedict. No particular prayer is prescribed since wearing the medal on your body is in itself is a continual silent prayer. These medals even have a prayer of exorcism imprinted directly on the front.

OTHER SACRAMENTALS

The Miraculous Medal is one of my favorites. Mary promised to grant many graces to those who wear the miraculous medal with confidence. One of those promises was protection from evil.

Rosaries are protective when worn around the neck as well as crucifixes and crosses. We also have available to us scapulars and cords belonging to particular Saints. Out of all the cords, the cord of St. Philomena offers wearers protection from evil. This cord is worn like a belt or around the neck. The faithful wear the cord of St. Philomena in her honor, to be protected in times of need, and to obtain healing of the body and spirit. You can also hang the cord over doorways for protection.

HOLY WATER

This water forms a protective barrier between you and any entity that means to cause harm. I like to keep mine in a small spray bottle since it's easier to use, and I'm also able to adjust the amount of spray needed. This is a very common and well known sacramental that should be kept in supply. Holy Water can be sprayed all over yourself or in the home for protection.

AMPARO

Two of my favorite protective Saints are St. Michael and San Cipriano (Patron Saint magicians, sorcerers, and witchcraft). Before working with Santa Muerte I will light a candle for both of these Saints and pray to them to place a protective shield around me. Next I will take two prayer cards or two printed photos of the Saints and sandwich my own photo in between them. The stack is then placed under each of their candles.

PRAYERS FOR PROTECTION

PSALM 1

PROTECTION FROM ENEMIES

Blessed is the man who does not walk in the counsel of the wicked or stand in the way of sinners or sit in the seat of mockers.

But his delight is in the law of the Lord, and on his law he meditates day and night.

He is like a tree planted by streams of water,

which yields its fruit in season and whose leaf does not wither.

Whatever he does prospers.

Not so the wicked! They are like chaff that the wind blows away.

Therefore the wicked will not stand in the judgment, nor sinners in the assembly of the righteous.

For the Lord watches over the way of the righteous, but the way of the wicked will perish.

PSALM 11

TO DRIVE AWAY DEMONS AND TO OVERCOME ENEMIES

In the Lord I take refuge.

How then can you say to me: "Flee like a bird to your mountain.

For look, the wicked bend their bows;

they set their arrows against the strings to shoot from the shadows at the upright in heart.

When the foundations are being destroyed, what can the righteous do?"

The Lord is in his holy temple; the Lord is on his heavenly throne.

He observes the sons of men; his eyes examine them.

The Lord examines the righteous, but the wicked and those who love violence his soul hates.

On the wicked he will rain fiery coals and burning sulfur; a scorching wind will be their lot.

For the Lord is righteous, he loves justice; upright men will see his face

PSALM 16

PROTECTION FROM SATANIC PROCESSIONS

Keep me safe, O God, for in you I take refuge.

I said to the Lord, "You are my Lord; apart from you I have no good thing."

As for the saints who are in the land, they are the glorious ones in whom is all my delight.

The sorrows of those will increase who run after other gods. I will not pour out their libations of blood or take up their names on my lips.

Lord, you have assigned me my portion and my cup; you have made my lot secure.

The boundary lines have fallen for me in pleasant places; surely I have a delightful inheritance.

I will praise the Lord, who counsels me; even at night my heart instructs me.

I have set the Lord always before me. Because he is at my right hand, I will not be shaken.

Therefore my heart is glad and my tongue rejoices; my body also will rest secure, because you will not abandon me to the grave, nor will you let your Holy One see decay.

You have made known to me the path of life;

you will fill me with joy in your presence,

with eternal pleasures at your right hand.

PSALM 23

FOR PROTECTION

The Lord is my shepherd, I shall not be in want.

He makes me lie down in green pastures, he leads me beside quiet waters, he restores my soul. He guides me in paths of righteousness for his name's sake.

Even though I walk through the valley of the shadow of death, I will fear no evil, for you are with me; your rod and your staff, they comfort me.

You prepare a table before me in the presence of my enemies.

You anoint my head with oil; my cup overflows.

Surely goodness and mercy will follow me all the days of my life, and I will dwell in the house of the Lord forever.

ST MICHAEL PROTECTION PRAYER

Holy Michael the Archangel, defend us in battle.
Be our protection against the wickedness and snares of the devil.
May God rebuke him, we humbly pray;
and do thou, O Prince of the heavenly hosts,
by the power of God,
thrust into hell Satan and all the other evil spirits
who prowl through the world
seeking the ruin of souls. Amen.

ARMY OF PROTECTION

I now call Michael the Archangel and his army of angels
to surround, fill and protect me.
I praise God for all of his heavenly angels.
I call them forth now and release them
to surround and fill us with God's power and blessings,
in the name of the Father, and the Son, and the Holy Spirit.
In the name of Jesus Christ,
I command all human spirits to be bound
to the confines of the cemetery.
I command all inhuman spirits
to go where Jesus Christ tells you to go
for it is he who commands you. Amen

POWERFUL PROTECTION

Heavenly Father, through the death and resurrection
of your Holy Son, Jesus of Nazareth,
we ask that you send your Holy Mother
along with the Guarding Angels
to descend upon my home (business or workplace)
to guard my family (friends and co-workers)

against the plots of Satan,
evil spirits and those who wish me harm
so that this building is forever consecrated
to the Sacred and Immaculate Hearts
from this day forward. Amen.

PRAYER FOR PROTECTION AGAINST DEMONS

O Mary, powerful Virgin,
you are the mighty and glorious protector of the Church
you are the marvelous help of Christians
in the midst of my anguish, my struggles and my distress,
defend me from the power of the enemy,
and at the hour of my death,
receive my soul into paradise. Amen.

SANTA MUERTE PROTECTION

Santisima Muerte, ruler over all spirits
Drape me with your protective cloak
Ban any evil spirit
From intruding upon this space
In which I use to only work
In closeness with you and your power
Just your gaze in their direction
Will keep them away
Watch over me at this moment
And keep me safe from all harm
Cast your blinding fire
Into the eye of anyone
Who looks in my direction
With ill intentions
And give me the strength
To overcome my enemies

WRITING PETITIONS AND REQUESTS

Most times, practitioners will write out their desire, intention, or request on paper. Short descriptive letters are also written to the Santa Muerte asking in detail what they want and also for drawing and blessing the work they perform. Names are written to bring the energy of life to your workspace and to candles used in spellwork. Written words carry power. Writing out a request is a way of sealing and empowering the outcome the practitioner seeks. It's also a way of presenting the practitioners desire it to the spirit realm.

Parchment paper is among the most popular paper used in spellwork although there are other types of paper that can be used. Virgin parchment is a term that refers to a paper that has never been used before and has been blessed for ritual purposes.

Historically, parchment was made from animal skin and there was a complex ritual to bless and kill the animal and then prepare the skin. For millennia, parchment was used as an archival writing surface. The word "parchment" (vellum) was derived from the Latin word Permagon -
where parchment is said to have been invented around the second century BC. Parchment documents have been found that date as far back as Egypt's Old Kingdom (about 2500BC) though the exact history of parchment is somewhat nebulous.

Vellum is a word generally used interchangeably with parchment. However, vellum refers to a particularly fine type of parchment, usually made from the skin of a very young animal, especially calfskin, and is often rendered clear and white.
Parchment and vellum both make excellent book binding materials for their strength and longevity with low elasticity. Parchment was considered a superior writing surface and

continues to be an expensive item. Many animal and nature activists who practice spellwork feel that it is wrong to use the skin of an animal; others feel it is wrong to cut down a tree for producing paper. Either way, real parchment can still be found, but fine paper works just as well and does cost less.

If you have a creative side, you can always make your own paper and incorporate different herbs, oils, or powders into the paper itself. The internet is loaded with recipes for making your own paper. In my opinion, the more handmade items you use in spellwork, the better and more powerful the outcome. Plus if you're a greenie (frugal, or one who likes to pinch pennies) making your own paper is cost effective and you can recycle your paper trash at the same time.

Just cleanse and purify it when it's made.

Parchment paper can be expensive, especially if you do a lot of petitioning in writing. Another paper that can be used is rice paper. Rice paper is paper made from the pith of the rice plant, or from a variety of other plants including mulberry and hemp. It is traditionally associated with Asian arts and crafts, and it has been used for centuries in Japan and China as a material for writing. This kind of paper has a distinctive texture, and the slightly translucent paper of most rice paper makes it appear to glow in a way that other papers do not. This sort of gives the appearance of "mystery". Most crafts and paper stores sell it.

True rice paper actually made from the rice plant, is fairly rare since most "rice paper" on the market is actually made from mulberry, and it tends to be smooth, slightly crackly, and rather thin. This mulberry paper is often dyed, or it may be made with vegetative inclusions for more texture. It is also known as washi, which is a name for high-grade handmade specialty paper.

Mulberry fiber may also be blended with fibers from other

plants, including rice, to make rice paper. Another type of rice paper is made from the fibers of the Tetrapanax papyifer, the "rice paper plant," a tree native to Taiwan.

Colored construction paper can also be used which can match the candle or a color related to the practitioners desire, such as red for matters of the heat or green for financial matters. Other times paper torn from brown paper bags can be used.

When I'm writing a petition to sending evil away, breaking witchcraft, or reversing a curse I like to have uneven edges. This isn't necessary. I know several people who prefer cut straight edges.
To achieve this I just tear the paper freehand making sure there are no straight edges around the perimeter of the paper. For everything else I use straight, crisp edges which I cut with a special pair of scissor which has been dedicated to my spiritual work.

Pay extra attention to your written petitions and write them out in detail. Writing petitions is not merely jotting down your desire or writing down someone's name. The actual writing of a petition is part of the spellwork itself and needs plenty time, attention, and thought. Be clear on what it is you would like.

If your goal is to find a new and better job you should write it out in as much detail as possible.
Include such things as the hours you want to work, the days you want off, you ideal pay, miles from home, room for growth, and whatever else you see your ideal job being. The same goes for love matters. If you want to attract new love towards you write how tall your ideal partner should be, weight, financial status, age, etc.

When you are writing names of people always include their

entire birth given name if possible.

This name holds their true essence. Nicknames are not as powerful since these names hold no real essence of the person.

When writing women's names try to include her maiden name since this name is part of her true identity. When writing a woman's name that is married, divorced, widowed, or otherwise going by a name other than her maiden, you would still include her maiden name. Her name would then be written as First, Middle, Maiden, Assumed (last name she is currently going by). For instance a woman named Martha Catherine Smith at birth marries and uses her husbands name Jones. Her name would be written as Martha Catherine Smith Jones. Her maiden name would always come before her assumed name.

Using Mrs., Miss, or Ms is less important but there are some people who like to include these tag names when writing petitions. The problem is that many people don't know the difference between these tags; you hear people speaking these terms incorrectly all the time. So if you're going to use them, use them correctly. Mrs. is used to refer to a married or widowed woman; Miss is used to refer to an unmarried female; and Ms. is used when referring to a woman that you know nothing about. Here you don't know if she's married, single or widowed. Like I said, these tags are not necessary when writing women's names.

On the other hand, when it comes to men's names it is important to include tag names. If the man is a Jr., Sr., the 1st, 2nd, 3rd, etc... These tags should always be included in your petition. Tag names given to men separate them from their father and sons, plus when a man has a tag name it was usually given to him at birth (or after having a male child) and is part of his essence.

When writing a petition paper you have to be in full concentration. Visualize the reality of your desire. If you're working a candle to attract new love towards you, see it playing out in your mind. See yourself meeting your ideal partner, the fun you have doing things together, getting married, having children.....whatever your desired outcome is.....visualize the reality of it in your minds eye. Focus and concentrate on this reality as hard and as intensely as you can.

When working a spell to dominate someone you should always write your name or a command over theirs. This gives you power over them. You see this same type of dominance in the animal world. When an animal wants dominance over another, the stronger one is always on top, holding the other one down. It's the same concept in spellwork.

If you want to dominate someone or something positively you turn your written petition paper to the right and if you want to dominate negatively you turn your petition paper to the left. Also, if you plan on folding your written petition you want to fold it "towards" you when your goal is to "attract" and fold it away from you when your goal is to "remove". Towards yourself is positive and away from yourself is negative.

For instance, say you want to make Martha Catherine Smith fall in love with you. You would write her name on the petition paper first. Since you want to make her fall in love with you this would be something "positive", something you "want". So you would write her name first, turn the paper to the right and write your name or your command over hers.....forming a "cross".

Now let's say you want to make Martha Catherine Smith

leave you alone. Since you want to make her "leave" this would be something "negative", something you "don't want" (her). So you would write her name first, turn the paper to the left and write your name or your command over hers.....forming a "cross". When you want to "attract", "draw", or "bring" you turn your petition paper to the right. When you want to "remove", "lessen", or "send away" you turn your petition paper to the right.....always forming a cross over their name.

So what do you write with? That's up to you. I know people who are successful spell workers that use colored pencils for all their petition papers. They like using them because these pencils are usually not lead based and they come in different colors. They use the color related to the work they are doing....red for love, green for money, etc. Others use regular ink pens with the color ink they need.

There are also spiritual inks that can be purchased or made. If you decide to make them yourself you have the advantage of not only knowing it's a good quality ink, since you know what you made it from, but you can also add herbs, oils, or small pieces of stone to your ink to add power to your spell.

Bat's blood ink is made from dragon's blood resin and other ingredients. It can be used for spellwork related to binding, jinxing, banishing, revenge, cursing, and hexing.

Dragon's blood ink is made from the resin of a palm tree. You can use this ink for protection or to return a lost love, impotence, manipulation, and for writing spells and making spiritual amulets and talismans.

Dove's blood ink is made from dragon's blood resin, rose, cinnamon, and other ingredients. It can be used for making amulets and talismans, love, fertility, spiritual blessing, and drawing things to you.

Seraph's ink is made from real saffron, frankincense, and other ingredients. It can be used for protection, guidance, and positive work.

GIVING LIFE TO CANDLES

BAPTIZING CANDLES

Baptizing and giving life to the candle is done after inscriptions and carving and before sectioning and dressing. Some people prefer to give the candle its life after everything else has been completed but if you wait to give life to the candle last, after everything else has been done, you are forced to work the candle spell right away. Waiting to dress the candle after the baptism gives you the opportunity to save the baptized candle for later use.

There are several things you can do to add life to your spell candle when it involves a person.

One way is to go through a baptism ceremony. The ceremony is performed almost like a real ceremony a baby is given at birth in a church setting by a priest.

By baptizing a candle you are creating life within it. The candle then takes on the spirit and essence of that person it is baptized to, giving you domination over it. Once baptized the candle is therefore a true representation of that person.

For this ceremonial ritual you will need:
Ceremony table
White table cloth
Incense (I like to use church incense)
Charcoal disk
Censer or heat proof container for burning incense
Matches
Holy water

Shallow bowl to hold water
Picture of the person
1 white candle to represent yourself
1 white candle to represent the person
1 white candle to represent God
1 white candle to represent guides
4 candle holders
Salt
Shallow bowl to hold salt
Virgin olive oil
Shallow bowl to hold oil
Crucifix
Candle to be baptized
Copy of these instructions for you to read during the ceremony

Baptism Table Setup
A) Candle to represent yourself B) Candle to represent the person C) Incense D) Candle for your spirit guides E) Blessed Salt F) Bowl of Holy Water G) Blessed Oil H) Candle to God
I) Photo of person J) Crucifix

Above is the setup for ritual baptism of a candle. Do not use your altar surface for the ceremony, a typical altar usually doesn't provide enough room for this ritual. Instead, you should have a separate ceremony table which is set up in front of your main altar. If possible, the ceremony should be performed on a Sunday since this is the day baptisms are usually done in the Church.
The crucifix is there for spiritual protection and blessing but isn't physically handled during the ceremony.

The candle that represents the person (B in the drawing) is not the same candle you will be baptizing. This candle is lit and represents the person's spirit during the ceremony. The candle you will be baptizing is the one you will use in your spellwork whenever you want to influence that person. Once the candle is baptized you can put it away and save it for spellwork at another time or you can use it right away. The effect of the baptism will still be as strong as when the ceremony is first performed.

Another thing to keep in mind is that if your spellwork calls for more than one candle to be used, say you are going to work on this person over a period of several weeks, you might want to baptize several of them at once. That way you don't have to go through the ceremony each time.

Drape the ceremony table with a clean white table cloth. This cloth can be personally decorated or it can be left pain white without decorations. Decorations are not necessary but it does add visual interest. I have a white ceremony cloth which I have sewn crystal beads around the edge and on the four corners I have embroidered crosses in white satin embroidery thread. It's visually appealing and I feel contributes more of an effect to the real church setting. If you decide to decorate your ceremony cloth keep all decorations white. There shouldn't be much color.

Once you have the table set up you should light a candle to Santa Muerte and recite a prayer of protection. This protection candle is not part of the ceremony table so place it away from the table you will be working the baptism on. The best place to light this candle is on her altar. All items used in the baptism should be previously cleansed and blessed.

To begin the baptism, light candle H, the candle to God. With your hands in a prayer position pray.....

"Lord Jesus, You are the Light of the world: we praise you,

and ask you to guide our steps each day. Bless this candle, and let it always remind us that you are our Light in darkness, our protector in danger, and our saving Lord at all times. Lord Jesus, we praise you and give you glory, for you are Lord for ever and ever. Amen."

Make the sign of the cross over the front of your body.

Now light candle A, candle that represents yourself. Hands in a prayer position and pray....

"Lord Jesus Christ, Son of the living God, bless this candle at our request. By virtue of the holy cross, Lord, pour upon it the virtue of your heavenly blessing. You have given it to mankind to drive away the dark. May it receive such blessing that wherever it may be lit or placed, the princes of darkness may depart and be afraid and fly in fear from those houses with all their helpers. Nor may they dare again to trouble or bother those who serve you, almighty God, who live and are King for ever and ever. May this candle serve to represent myself in Holy protection. Amen.

Make the sign of the cross over the front of your body.

Now light the ritual incense. I prefer to use Church Incense, also called "Gloria Incense". Both of these incenses are sold loose so you will need a charcoal disk to burn them. I have never seen them sold in the form of sticks or cones. Censors are safe for burning incense when a charcoal disk is used. If you do not have a sensor you are going to need a heat proof container. I suggest using one of those glass cooking skillets with a handle. The charcoal disks get very hot and will melt through most containers, so make sure the container you use can withstand a tremendous amount of heat. Also if you're not using a sensor make sure to place the incense container on a large slab of rock or another heat proof surface to avoid burning your table surface or your

ceremony cloth.
When the incense is ignited and begins to smoke, hold your right hand, slightly cupped, over the incense and pray......

"Let us pray to our Father in heaven, who has given us this incense for our use. (moment of silence). Blessed are you, Lord God, king of the universe: you have made all things for your glory. Bless this incense and grant that we may use it in spiritual power. Father, we praise you through Christ our Lord. Amen"

Make the sign of the cross over the incense.
(if the incense goes out before the ceremony is over just add more to the hot charcoal) Now bless the salt......
This is the prayer used by the Catholic Church for the blessing of salt. Take the bowl of salt and hold it in your left hand. Hold your right hand, slightly cupped, over the salt and recite this prayer......

"Almighty God, we ask you to bless this salt, as once you blessed the salt scattered over the water by the prophet Elisha. Grant this through Christ our Lord. Amen."

Make the sign of the cross over the salt.

Now bless the oil....
To bless the oil that will be used. You are going to use virgin olive oil so pour a small amount into a shallow bowl. Hold the bowl in your left hand. Hold your right hand, slightly cupped, over the oil and recite this prayer......

"Lord God Almighty, before whom the hosts of angels stand in awe, and whose heavenly service we acknowledge; may it please you to regard favorably and to bless and hallow this creature, oil, which by your power has been pressed from the juice of olives. Through Christ our Lord. Amen."

Make the sign of the cross over the oil.

Now light candle D, which represents your spirit guides and pray.....

"I call upon my spirit guides assigned to me at birth and to those spirits who surround me with their help. I call upon you to assist me in this moment of ceremony and all the days of my life.

Lead me in the direction needed to obtain what I seek. Make your powerful presence be known at this moment. Conquer the spirit of (person's name) to occupy this (these) candle(s) give it life and obedience under my command."

Now light candle B, the one which represents the person's spirit and pray.....

"Spirit of (person's name) I dominate you."

Now take the candle(s) that will be baptized and hold it over the bowl of Holy Water in your left hand. With your right hand cup some of the water in the palm of your hand and pour it over the candle and pray.....

"I baptize you as (person's name) in the name of the Father, and of the Son and of the Holy Spirit."

Do this three times.

Now pour one more handful of water over the candle and pray.....

"By way of life giving water, I baptize you (name of person), I give you life, and I dominate you."

Now take the blessed salt and with your right hand, sprinkle some of the salt over the candle and pray......

"By the way of the land, I baptize you (person's name), I give you life, and I dominate you."

Pass the candle through the smoke of the incense and pray.....

"By the way of the air you breathe, I baptize you (name of person), I give you life, and I dominate you."

Now hold the candle in both hands in front of the lit candle that represents the person's spirit and pray....

"By the way of fire, I baptize you (person's name), I give you life, and I dominate you.

Now take the persons picture and place it on the table in front of the bowl of water. Lay the baptized candle on top of the photo. Dip the thumb of your right hand into the blessed oil and make the sign of the cross over the candle. As you are doing this pray....

"This baptism is sealed."

You are finished. Here you can pray in your own words asking Santa Muerte to take control and grant you domination.

If you plan on using the candle at a later date make sure to properly store the candle. The candle should be wrapped in a soft white fabric. White represents purity, the white is to keep the purity of the candle after baptism until it is used in a candle spell. Until the candle is actually used it's like a baby.....new and pure, and should be treated that way. The fabric is to keep the dust and other particles off the candle itself. Place the wrapped candles in a lidded box. This is to keep the fabric white, without dust. Purity does not mean dirty white. A shoebox works well for this purpose. Store the candle in a cool place. This is to not only keep the candle from distorting from heat exposure but also to nurture the purity of the baptism. You wouldn't expose a new baby to high heat. After the baptism it's advised that you perform a good spiritual cleansing on yourself.

Adding Personal Energy

If you prefer not to go through the ritual baptism you can still give life to your spell candle in other ways which we will talk a little about in this section.

Another way to add life to a spell candle besides carving a name on the side is to dig out a small hole in the bottom of the candle and fill the hole with small personal items belonging to the person. Here you have several options. If you can get any of the person's hair or nail clippings these can be placed inside the hole and wax melted over it to seal the items inside. Also body fluids, such as blood, semen, bodily oils, and sweat can be collected on tiny pieces of tissue and placed inside the candle.

If you have access to any of the person's clothing which has not been previously washed, these items contain the energy of the person and have some of their sweat or body oils on the fabric.
You can cut a tiny piece from the clothing to place inside the candle. Keep the fabric extra small since you won't be able to fit larger cuttings inside the hole. If all you can get is fabric the size of a pencil lead that's really all that's needed, the energy is there. Worn fabric samples can be taken off of worn socks, shirts, pants, shoes, underwear, caps, etc... And if you take just the slightest amount from an article of clothing they probably won't even notice it.

You can also copy and print their picture and size it down really small. This can be rolled up and placed inside the hole as well. If you don't have a photo of the person you can simply write their name on a paper along with any other personal information such as birth date and use that instead of an actual photo. Dirt taken from where the person has walked and left a footprint can be used to give life to the candle too. The possibilities of obtaining personalized items are endless if you look around.

FIXING GLASS ENCASED CANDLES

The Star of David is a six-pointed star which is also known as the Hexagram, the Shield of David, Solomon's Seal, and Magen David. It's made of two interlocking triangles. The six points of the Star of David symbolize God's rule over the universe in all six directions: North, South, East, West, Up and Down.

Because of its geometric symmetry, the hexagram has been a popular symbol in many cultures from earliest times. Anthropologists claim that the triangle pointing downward represents female sexuality, and the triangle pointing upward, male sexuality; thus, their combination symbolizes unity and harmony. In alchemy, the two triangles symbolize "fire" and "water"; together, they represent the reconciliation of opposites.

Legends connect this symbol with the Seal of Solomon, the magical ring used by King Solomon to control demons and spirits. Although the original ring was inscribed with the Tetragrammaton, the sacred Four-Letter Name of God, medieval amulets imitating this ring substituted the hexagram or pentagram (five-pointed stare), often accompanied by rampant lions, for the sacred Name.

The hexagram first appears as a magical symbol in the early

Middle Ages, especially in Muslim and Christian countries, and was used on notary seals as well as for architectural decoration on
churches. It appears that the hexagram was employed even earlier by the Karraite Judah Hadassi in the mid-12th century in connection with amulets and names for God. However, at this time it did not symbolize either God or the Jewish people; its precise meaning is unclear, but scholars have suggested that it suggested God's protecting power, hence the association with a "shield".

The star was also employed in Kabbalah at this time; the ten sefirot were arranged within the six-pointed star and it was used in amulets. It further appears that the hexagram and pentagram were used interchangeably until this period, and then the six-pointed star gained favor, as it was associated with the notion of a "shield" of God and taken to have magical powers when used as an amulet.

From the 14th century through the 18th century, the terms "shield of David" and "seal of Solomon" were used in magical texts indiscriminately though the hexagram ascended in popularity as the pentagram diminished in popularity. It is in this context that the Prague Jewish community chose to use the hexagram as its symbol when King Charles IV granted them the privilege of having their own flag in 1354.

Amongst Christians, the pentagram has been used as a protective amulet, and has been used to represent the Star of Bethlehem which appeared at the time of the birth of Jesus. It was also used by the Emperor Constantine, who is associated with the popularization of the cross as a seal.

The Star is believed to offer one protection, bring luck and give one power and strength. Glass encased candles can be fixed using this powerful symbol.

Take the glass encased candle and with your ritual knife (ritual knife: you should have a knife used specifically for spellwork. This can be a pocket knife, a dagger, or any other knife reserved only for spiritual work) draw the Star of David over the top of the wax. Make it as large as the diameter of the glass so that you can poke holes in the wax without breaking the lines of the star.

If your candle is going to be for the purpose of "drawing" or "attracting" something, begin drawing the star towards the right. This is the direction to ATTRACT. If your intention is to
"remove", or "rid" something, begin drawing the star towards your left. This is the direction to SEND AWAY.

Once you have the star carved into the top of the candle use a brass rod to poke three deep holes into the top of the wax. Other objects can be used to make the holes but brass is a very powerful
metal which is related to protection and power, so if you can, use a brass rod. Make sure to poke the holes inside the smaller triangles so that you don't break the lines of the star.

Now you can add some spiritual oil related to the job your doing. If your candle is going to be used for lover purposes, use the appropriate love oil. If your candle is going to be used for money purposes, use the appropriate money oil.

Carefully pour nine drops of your chosen oil divided into each hole, no more. Nine is the number for Santa Muerte. If you add too little oil the candle won't be fixed strong enough and if you use too much oil you will have a hard time keeping your candle lit.

Once you have poured your oils, spray the outside of the glass with Holy Water, allowing it to dry on its own. Recite

3 Our Fathers, 3 Hail Mary's and 3 Glory Be's (prayers follow) making the sign of the Cross over the top of the candle with your right hand. Finish by placing some of the oil in the form of the Cross on the bottom of the candle.

Our Father
Our Father who art in Heaven
Hallowed be thy name
Thy kingdom come, thy will be done
On earth as it is in Heaven
Give us this day, our daily bread
As we forgive us our trespasses
As we forgive those who trespass against us
And lead us not into temptation but deliver us from evil
For thine is the kingdom
And the power
And the glory
Forever and ever amen

Hail Mary
Hail Mary full of grace
Blessed art thou amongst women
And blessed is the fruit of thy womb, Jesus
Holy Mary, Mother of god
Pray for us sinners
Now and at the hour of our death Amen

Glory Be
Glory be to the Father, to the Son, and to the Holy Spirit
As it was in the beginning, is now, and ever shall be
Amen

A COLLECTION OF SANTA MUERTE PRAYERS

Opening and Closing Prayers

Our Father

Our Father, who art in Heaven, hallowed be thy name. Thy kingdom come, Thy will be done, on earth as it is in heaven. Give us this day our daily bread, and forgive us our trespasses, as we forgive those who trespass against us. And lead us not into temptation, but deliver us from evil. Amen.

Hail Mary (X3)

Hail Mary, full of grace, the Lord is with thee. Blessed art thou among women and blessed is the fruit of thy womb, Jesus. Holy Mary, Mother of God pray for us sinners, now and at the hour of death. Amen.

Glory Be

Glory be to the Father, to the Son, and to the Holy Spirit, as it was in the beginning, is now, and ever shall be, world without end. Amen.

St. Michael

St. Michael, the Archangel, defend us in our day of battle. Be our safeguard against the wickedness and snares of the Devil. May God rebuke him, we humbly pray, and do thou, O Prince of the Heavenly Host, by the power of God, thrust into Hell Satan and the other evil spirits who prowl through the world seeking the ruin of souls. Amen.

Invocational Prayer

Almighty God, before your Divine Presence, in the name of the Father, Son, and Holy Spirit, we ask permission to invoke the Santisima Muerte. Holy and Powerful Mother, at this moment we beg for your presence and intervention.

Through the great power, which God has given you, we beg of you to hear our prayers and grant us all the favors we ask of you until the last day, hour, and moment when the Divine Majesty shall call us before his presence. Santisima Muerte, beloved of our hearts, do not abandon us without your protection. In the name of the Father, the Son, and the Holy Spirit. Amen.

Ending Prayers
In the name of the Father, the Son, and the Holy Spirit. Santisima Muerte, Our Most Holy Mother, we beseech you lovingly to protect those who carry your prayers and devoutly honor you. Cover them with your mantle, and guard them with your scythe, that their enemies may not have dominion over them. Protect them from bad luck, disease, and envy; witchcraft, hexes, and curses; lightning, fires, and earthquakes; demons, evil spirits, and phantoms; evil eyes, evil hearts, and evil minds; cover them, oh Holy Mother, so that no evil can see them, no evil can touch them, and no evil can follow them. In the name of the Father, the Son, and the Holy Spirit. Amen. (pray 3 Our Fathers)

PRAYERS FOR LA BLANCA

Prayer for La Blanca
Santisima Muerte, La Blanca, Most Holy Death of the White Robe, eldest of the Three, you who sit at the right hand of God, hear our prayers. Glorious Huesuda, you who grant the peaceful death of old age and heal the sick, through the great power, which God has given you, we ask you to remove all sickness from our lives. Niña Blanca, with your holy scales, bring balance to our bodies, minds, and souls and protect us from all illness. Santisima Muerte La Blanca, Holiest of Archangels, cover us with your pure robe, we pray. In the name of the Father, the Son, and the Holy Spirit. Amen.

Prayer for Health

Santisima Muerte, La Blanca, you have the power to heal all illnesses or inflict them. We come before you, begging for your assistance. You know the cure for all sickness and can administer it to free men from their suffering. Oh Holy Mother, we beg you to have compassion on us (or for whom you are praying) and grant us (or him/her) a miracle, for the pains that we (or he/she) suffer(s). Amen.

Prayer for Cleansing/Uncrossing

Santisima Muerte, La Blanca, with your very presence you can break all hexes and evil spells. We ask, oh Holy Mother, that with your scythe you separate from us (or for whom you are praying) from that which crosses, that which causes illness, and that which is unclean. Purify us (or him/her), oh Miraculous Muerte, by the great power, which God has given you. In the name of the Father, the Son, and the Holy Spirit. Amen.

Hourglass Prayer

Santisima Muerte, La Blanca, you have the power to grant the peaceful death of old age. La Huesuda, we beg that you intercede on our behalf and grant unto us (or for whom you are praying) the precious gift of more time in this life. Please, merciful Archangel of God, turn again your hourglass for us (or him/her) so that we (or he/she) may have the honor of bearing witness to your mercy and power. In the name of the Father, the Son, and the Holy Spirit. Amen.

PRAYERS FOR LA ROJA

Prayer for La Roja

Santisima Muerte, La Roja, Most Holy Death of the Red Robe, born from the first love, hear our prayers. Niña Roja, you whose powers over matters of the heart are beyond compare, know our desires and grant us what we ask. Glorious Madrina, you who work within the world, through the great power, which God has given you, we ask that you assist us with our many needs. Santisima Muerte La Roja, Holiest of Archangels, protect us from the deaths of your robe. In the name of the Father, the Son, and the Holy Spirit. Amen.

Prayer for Money
Oh Holy Mother la Muerte, in your hands all things shall come to dust. No gold or silver can turn your gaze, nor block your path. You cast it aside as dust, just as you will do to our flesh when the Divine Majesty calls. Oh Holy Mother, place us in the path of gold. Oh Holy Mother, place us in the path of silver. Let prosperity come to us, but assist us to always remember that wealth is only a useful tool, when one does not become its slave. Amen.

Prayer for Employment
Santisima Muerte, you know what lies down all paths, and can see beyond all roads. Lead us down a prosperous path, that we may find employment that will be befitting the vocation which the Divine Majesty has ordained for mus. Assist us in this necessity, for in God we believe, and in you we confide. Amen.

Petition Prayer
Santisima Muerte, La Roja, beloved of our hearts, do not abandon us without your protection. Oh Holy and Immaculate Being of Light, we beg of you to look with compassion upon us and our petition. Oh Holy Angel of God, who shall come to each and everyone one of us, who has the power to remove the soul from the flesh, we beg of you to grant the petition we place before thee. (Mention your petition or place it on her altar.) In the name of the Father, the Son, and the Holy Spirit. Amen.

PRAYERS FOR LA NEGRA

Prayer for La Negra
Santisima Muerte, La Negra, Most Holy Death of the Black Robe, born from the first murder, you who are the hottest

of the Three, hear our prayers. Powerful Muerte, enthroned as queen of the witches, only you can descend into Hell and not be touched by the demons and spirits that reside there. Fearsome Mother, you grant the strongest protection from curses, witchcraft, and evil spirits, and the diseases of the world are also your children, who you send and take way at will. Grant us your protection, La Negra, and cover us with your shadowy robe. This we ask in the name of the Father, the Son, and the Holy Spirit. Amen.

Prayer for Protection

Santisima Muerte, La Negra, hold us in your powerful arms, and shadow us with your mantle. Protect us from all harm, let no evil befall us. To those who wish us harm: Blind their eyes, so they can't see us, Bind their arms, so they can't grab us, Bind their feet, so they can't follow us, Stop their ears, so they can't hear us, and Cloud their minds so they'll forget us. Amen.

Prayer to Remove Evil

Oh Santisima Muerte, Our Blessed Lady of the Land of the Shades, we beseech your presence and intervention. With your cloak, cover us with the mantle of your holy protection, and with your scythe, cut down all evil that presents itself in our lives, our homes, our jobs, and our paths. Through the great power, which God has given you, we ask that you banish all evil spirits, evil spells, witchcraft, hexes, curses, evil eyes, evil minds, and evil hearts from our presence. Our Most Holy Mother, look through the darkness that surrounds us, and remove all these evils. Amen.

Prayer Against Enemies (The Prayer of the Scythe)

Santisima Muerte, La Negra, we come before you, kneeling at your feet, imploring your force, power, and presence against those who intend to destroy us. Our Mother, we ask that you be our shield and protection against the evil our enemies may send against us. With your scythe, cut through all obstacles that they have placed in our way, and open all doors they have closed to us. Clear our path, and lift us up beyond their reach, that their wickedness may not touch us.

Amen.

POWERFUL PRAYERS

TO ATTRACT THE SPIRIT OF A PERSON

Spirit, body and soul of (name of person)
come because I am calling you, I dominate you
tranquility you will not have until you come surrendered at
my feet as I have this needle through the middle of this
candle
the thought of me will pass through the middle of your heart
so that you may forget whomever you have
and come to me when I call you.
(Repeat the above three times)
Angel of your day, angel of today,
Guardian Angel of (name of person)
bend the heart of (name of person)
so that he may forget anyone he has
and comes surrendered with love to my feet.
holy guardian angel of (name of person)
may you not allow (name of person) tranquility until he is at
my side.
Saint, oh Saint of my name and devotion that I tool
affection and desire That he be content with me is what
matters to me.
That he may love me, that I may love him
Return to me the affection of (name of person) who is gone.
Spirit, body, and soul of (name of person)
From this moment on he does not have joy,
Any desire other than for me
Spirit, body, and soul of (name of person)
That his love, his affection, his fortune,
His caresses, his kisses, everything of him be only for me.
Body and soul of (name of person)
You may not go to see nor love any other person other than
me.

Spirit of San Cipriano, bring him to me
Spirit of Santa Elena, bring him to me
Spirit of Santa Marta, bring him to me
Spirit of La Caridad de Cobre, bring him to me
Virgin de Covadonga, that you might bring me (name of person) Spirit of the light that illuminates the clouds of the souls
Light the brain of (name of person)
So that he remembers me and all that he has you may give me
Impulsed through your powers so that he be a slave to my love Tranquility give not until he is at my side.

FOR ADVICE

(this said before you go to bed)
Santisima Muerte as my body sleeps
My spirit will be among other spirits who roam
During my slumber I ask for your counsel
Whisper your words of advice into my ear
And allow me to remember upon awakening. Amen

FOR GOOD LUCK

Santa Muerte you know the secrets to great fortune
Please allow the path to fortune to bend in my direction
Permit me to partake in the ease that fortune brings
Santa Muerte remove all obstacles that keep good luck from finding me Smile upon me with the greatest of luck. Amen
(Recite 3 Our Fathers)

TO THE ALOE FOR HEALING

Most scared aloe vera, most loved by the powerful Santa Muerte Blessed Aloe, Holy Aloe, and Sacred Aloe
Through your virtue given to the Apostles
I beg that you extend this same virtue to me
Free me from evil, from sickness, from bad luck
Drive evil away from my home and free me

From enemies in all directions, keep me safe everywhere I may go
Supply me with plenty of well paying work, blessings, fortune and money Allow me to live with ease with the lease amount of effort
Keep me strong, famous, fortunate, joyous, and blessed
Banish from my path all obstacles that may keep me from success Through the divine virtue that God gave you, in God I believe, and in you I trust. Amen TO ATTRACT LOVE
Santa Muerte, matchmaker and help for the lonely
Hear my plea for companionship; hear my love for (person's name) I invoke you three times over and ask you to bring this person to me Santa Muerte help me, Santa Muerte help me, Santa Muerte help me Do not delay kind lady, bring the love of (persons name) forever at me feet Say three Our Fathers and this prayer daily.

LOVE

Jesus Christ the conqueror, who on the cross was conquered, conquer (name of person) that he be conquered by me (or name of person this prayer is for) in the name of the Lord if you are a fierce animal tame as a lamb, tame as the flower of rosemary; you must come; you ate bread, of him you gave me and through the most strong word that you gave me, I want you to bring me (or name of person this prayer is for) (name of person) that he be humbled, defeated at my feet to complete what to me he has offered Santisima Muerte, I beseech you lovingly inasmuch as Immortal God formed you with your great power over all mortals so that you might place them in the celestial sphere where they may enjoy a glorious day without night for all eternity and in the name of the Father, the Son and the Holy Spirit, I pray and I beseech you that you deign to be my protectress and that you concede all the favors that I ask of you until the last day, hour and moment in which your Divine Majesty commands to take me before your presence. Amen PROTECTION

Santa Muerte, I call upon you so that through your image you may free me from all dangers, either physical or from witchcraft and that through this sacred flame you purify my body
from all charms and curses.
Also grant me love, peace, and abundance. So be it.

JACULATORIA
Santa Muerte, dear to my heart do not leave me without protection
do not leave (name of person) one moment of tranquility
bother him every moment, mortify him
and disturb him so that he always thinks of me.
(Say 3 Our Fathers)

FOR MONEY
Santa Muerte, I ask for your blessings
To increase and better my finances
Help me to overcome all my debts
And to meet my household bills
Help me to have the means to feed my family
To cloth them and to provide medical needs
Relieve me of the pressure of financial difficulties
And grant us with enough left over
to enjoy the pleasures and luxuries in life. Amen

FOR A BUSINESS
Santa Muerte, I invite you to reside comfortably here
Within the walls of this business
Kindly remove all evil influences that may enter
Kindly remove all negativity which permeates these walls
Ensure that all customers who enter leave here with good things to say Bring this business in good standing with the community
Attract spending customers and increase my sales
And encourage customers to come here often

With your help Santa Muerte
My business will prosper and grow. Amen

FOR THANKS

Oh Santisima Muerte, my heart is full of gratitude
Thank you dearest power for all that you have done for me
Thank you for blessing me with what I have asked of you
Your image grows in my heart
Without your help I would have been helpless
Without your kindness I would not progress
From the bottom of my heart Santa Muerte
I thank you one hundred times over and again. Amen

FOR HEALTH

Santisima Muerte, powerful lady who God has given
immense power You who can be called upon for every need
known
Hear my call to you for help at this hour
I call upon you to heal my body from illness
From disease, weakness, fatigue, and from all disorders
But most of all Santa Muerte I call upon your help for
(mention your request) Amen

THE LOVE SPELL OF NINA NEGRA
YOU WILL NEED 9 RED CANDLES AND SAY THIS
PRAYER FOR 9 NIGHTS

Loving Nina Negra, spirit of happiness, I am in need of your
magic and power. May your enchantment be the
enchantment that realizes my desires and ends my solitude,
heartache and misfortune. With the purest and truest of
hearts and not desiring to cause or bring any harm, hurt or
misfortune to myself (Your Name) nor my beloved (Their
Name,) that their heart beat without interruption only for
me (your Name) in all directions.

Nina Negra, I ask you to turn (Their Name) in my favor so that they fall completely in love with me (Your Name,) and needs to have me with them now. Nina Negra, I beg of thee to go to where ever my beloved (Their Name) is and goes, and bring them to me (Your Name). Don't let them rest, sleep, be cheerful nor feel pleasure until they see me, speaks to me, and makes me their lover.

Nina Negra, I invoke thee by the powers of earth, for the presence of fire, for the inspiration of air, for the virtues of water, for the tears that I have shed over love, I invoke your spirit and that of the blessed souls so that you go to where ever (Their Name) is and bring their heart, body and soul and bind it to mine (Your Name) definitively. Have their spirit soak in the essence of my love so they will reciprocate their love to me in quadruple. May my beloved (Their Name) not desire any other person, that their thoughts and eyes only be about me (Your Name), I ask of thee, to make [Their Name] feel sorry for rejecting and being indifferent to me, and desire to see me and need me be to be their only lover.

Nina Negra, I ask of thee to move air, transform fire, form water, heal earth so the wheel turns and turns and turns and makes my beloved (their name) quickly come pursuing me (Your Name) crazily, humbly, passionately wanting to be by my side asking me to never let them go.

Nina Negra, I offer this candle to thee, knowing in my heart, that this will be granted to me and I thank you with all of my heart, spirit and soul. Amen

DAILY PRAYER OF THE BLESSED DEATH
Offer 1 white candle

Most holy death of my heart
My beloved queen

Save me under your mantle
Please grant me your many
Blessings, miracles and wonders
Because love and happiness are always
Present in my house and in my family
So that everything around me is harmonized
Open the roads for luck and fortune
Follow me and my family
Take away from me, my home and my family
All evil and unknown dangers and harms
Replace it with just good and joy
When I face the paths that all mortals
I have to face, I ask for your courage
And diaphanous to help go from day to day
Most holy death, I pray that you never abandon me or leave
me at any time
Please take away from me, my home and my loved ones
All the haters are jealous and envious
I pray that my prayers are always heard and
Granted by your divine blessings and holy intercession
Most Holy Death, my dear mother, keep me and my loved
ones
Always under your sole and total protection night and day
While we sleep and when we wake up to face a new day
On this day I praise her name and give my promise to all
Of my love, devotion. Faith and trust in your hands
Thanking you for all your blessings and protection
Amen

PRAYER OF SANTA MUERTE

Jesus Christ the Conqueror, who on the cross was conquered,
conquer (name of person) that he be conquered with me in the name of the Lord.
If you fierce animal, tame as a lamb, tame as the flower of rosemary, you must come, you ate bread, of him you gave me, and through the most strong word you gave me, I want you to bring me (name of person),

that he be humbled, defeated at my feet to complete what to me he has offered.

Santisima Muerte, I beseech you lovingly, inasmuch as immortal God formed you with your great power over all mortals so that you might place them in the celestial sphere where they may enjoy a glorious day without night for all eternity and in the name of the Father the Son and the Holy Spirit,

I pray and I beseech you that you deign to be my protectress and that you concede all the favors that I ask of you until the last day, hour and moment in which your divine majesty commands to take to before your presence. Amen.

SPELL PRAYER OF SANTA MUERTE

SAY THIS FOR 9 NIGHTS,STARTING ON A FRIDAY AT 9PM AND YOU NEED 9 WHITE TEA CANDLES,OFFER 1 CANDLE FOE EACH OF THE 9 NIGHTS

Santa Muerte I pray to thee and through Jesus Christ I implore you.

Santa Muerte I ask of thee, to remove this evil; remove these liars, traitors and enemies that surround me at this time

Santa Muerte I plead to thee, to remove all of this hatred, all of this envy and all of this salt, bad luck and misfortune from me, my home and my family

And instead place my feet on the path of luck, health, work and money

Santa Muerte I ask of you and the Lord Our Savior to hear my prayers...[say your need]

Santa Muerte, I beg of thee, to protect me with your shadow of goodness

Santa Muerte I kneel before you humbly and with a true heart. Through Christ Our Lord, Amen

SANTA MUERTE NOVENA
BEGINNING PRAYER FOR EVERY DAY

Santa Muerte, compassionate lady to all those who invoke you
Compassionate of those who suffer,
I bring my trouble to you through this novena,
I knee humbly at your feet and beg you to
Take my present need under your special protection
(make your request)

DAY ONE
Santa Muerte,
At your feet accept my request to invoke you daily,
not only for the success of my affairs and to be freed of
suffering, but also for your protection
(make your request)
Santa Muerte,
but obtain for me the grace that I ask of you today. Amen.
(say 3 Our Fathers)

DAY TWO
Santa Muerte, look upon me with kindness
I know I am not deserving of your help
But I come to you with a request because I have great faith
in you To you I address my prayers with confidence.
May I be granted your most speedy help
(make your request)
I stand in need at the present time.
(say 3 Our Fathers)

DAY THREE
Santa Muerte, God granted you such great power
to help those who call
take me under your special care and
grant this request I make at your feet
(make your request)
Hear my petition Santa Muerte
(say 3 Our Fathers)

DAY FOUR

Santa Muerte, I kneel in confidence at your feet,
To transform the urgent need that I place at your feet
My necessities, the cause of my tears, are
(make your request)
Santa Muerte, I beseech you to grant my prayer
(say 3 Our Fathers)

DAY FIVE

Santa Muerte, I have great faith in you
You are a powerful presence in my life
Hear my prayers Santa Muerte and come to my aid,
listen to my petition
(make your request)
make my confidence and fervor,
(say 3 Our Fathers)

DAY SIX

Santa Muerte,
Guardian of all who invoke your name
I beg you to obtain for me what I ask
(make your request)
Kneeling at your feet,
I beg you to help me in all that I ask
(say 3 Our Fathers)

DAY SEVEN

Santa Muerte,
You are my cure from this suffering
Be merciful Santa Muerte and grant for me
what I ask through this novena
(make your request)
(say 3 Our Fathers)

DAY EIGHT

Santa Muerte,
You name itself is powerful in the ears of those who hear

Look upon me with mercy and favor
I take refuge at your feet,
burdened with my present need
(make your request)
despise not my petition
but hear me and grant my prayer.
(say 3 Our Fathers)

DAY NINE
Santa Muerte, confiding in your kindness,
I come to you today for your help
I hope to serve you and honor you all my life
and to do all in my power to spread devotion to you.
(make your request)
deign to accept me as your devotee,
assist me in all the necessities that I place before your feet I
beg you to grant me this special favor
(say 3 Our Fathers) Amen.

3 Day Miracle Prayer of the Mother of Sorrows
You will need 3 black and 3 white candles and say this prayer
for 3 straight days at noon and midnight without fail and
your prayer will be granted

Merciful mother of sorrows
Look down on us with pit
Your faithful that cry out to thee in this valley of tears
We pray that you hear our prayers and help us to obtain the
comfort we need at this time
Merciful mother of sorrows
I pray that you hear my prayer on this day from heart
I seek your sole protection from the evil and harm that press
upon uei seek thy help so I do not fall before my enemy
Hold my hand and guide me on this path before me
I beg of thee to help me to grant this prayer with the
blessings of christ the grand redeemer
[say your need 3 times]..

Never cease not once to pray my request on my behalf
before the holy trinity
Helping me to gain vicatory over the snares and assaults
from the devil
Grant to me thy courage,power and strngth to be victorious
over this test of my faith
Intercede for me further my gear mother of sorrows muntil
the day I stand before st,peter to be judged
I place my whole entire being in thy hands and pray I never
fail before thee
I place all of my faith,hope love and trust upon thee to lift
me up to the lord
Amen

Prayer of the Blessed Mother
Blessed mother of impossible causes, never have it been
none for you to refuse your holy intercession before the
almighty God, you open your arms to accept all who
implore thy mercy, protection and kindness, my mother
look down upon this child of yours, broken, beaten tears
rolling down my face, I beg of you my mother, hear your
child pleading for your pity and compassion, and grant to
me this impossible favor that now place at your feet with a
humble and pure heart,..[say your favor]...And take my
prayers to be heard my the throne of the almighty god and
never cease once your holy and divine intercession until my
need is blessed and obtained, I place my whole entire being
in under thy sole protection from all crime, harm and evil,
in the Christ the grand redeemer ,I ask this with a pure
heart...Amen

LITANY OF SANTISIMA MUERTE
℣. Lord have mercy upon us.
℟. Lord have mercy upon us.
℣. Santsima Muerte, have mercy upon us.

℞. Santisima Muerte, have mercy upon us.

℣. Lord have mercy upon us.

℞. Lord have mercy upon us.

℣. God the Unknown Father,

℞. Shed Thy glory upon us.

℣. God the Incarnate Son,

℞. Shed Thy glory upon us.

℣. God the Sanctifier, the Spirit,

℞. Shed Thy glory upon us.

℣. Triune Godhead, three in one,

℞. Shed Thy glory upon us.

℣. Santisima Muerte,

℞. Hear us and be near us.

℣. Santisima Muerte,

℞. Have mercy upon us.

℣. Holy Mary, Mother of God,

℞. Have mercy upon us.

℣. Holy Mary, Our Lady of Guadalupe,

℞. Have mercy upon us.

℣. Archangel Michael,

℞. Give us thy strength.

℣. Archangel Gabriel,

℞. Give us thy knowledge.

℣. Archangel Raphael,

℞. Give us thy healing power.

℣. Archangel Uriel,

℞. Give us thine illumination.

℣. All the angels and archangels,

℞. Give us your aid.

℣. All the hosts of heaven,

℞. Pray for us.

℣. St. Joseph, spouse of the Blessed Virgin,

℟. Pray for us.
℣. Sts. Peter and Paul,
℟. Pray for us.
℣. Sts. Dominic and Francis,
℟. Pray for us.
℣. St. Juan de la Cruz,
℟. Pray for us.
℣. St. Mary Magdalene,
℟. Pray for us.
℣. Sts. Teresa and Catherine,
℟. Pray for us.
℣. All the soldiers of prayer and intercessors of heaven,
℟. Pray for us.
℣. All the great saints of Our Lord,
℟. Pray for us.
℣. O Most Precious and Divine Santisima Muerte, with Thy protective mantle,
℟. Cover us and the whole world, now and forever.
℣. Santisima Muerte, full of sanctity and compassion,
℟. Deliver us.
℣. Santisima Muerte, our strength and power,
℟. Deliver us.
℣. Santisima Muerte, eternal ally,
℟. Deliver us.
℣. Santisima Muerte, armor of God,
℟. Deliver us.
℣. Santisima Muerte, divine charity,
℟. Deliver us.
℣. Santisima Muerte, scourge of demons,
℟. Deliver us.
℣. Santisima Muerte, help of those who are bound,
℟. Deliver us.

℣. Santisima Muerte, Queen of Thy devotees,
℟. Deliver us.

℣. Divine Santisima Muerte, defender of the world,
℟. Deliver us.

℣. Santisima Muerte, true faith,
℟. Deliver us.

℣. Santisima Muerte, Queen of Charity,
℟. Deliver us.

℣. Divine Santisima Muerte, bestower of health,
℟. Save us.

℣. Divine Santisima Muerte, dignifier,
℟. Save us.

℣. Divine Santisima Muerte, strength of the children of God,
℟. Save us.

℣. Divine Santisima Muerte, commander of Thy warriors,
℟. Save us.

℣. Divine Santisima Muerte, companion of the angels of heaven,
℟. Save us.

℣. Divine Santisima Muerte, consolation of God the Father,
℟. Save us.

℣. Santisima Muerte, power of the Holy Spirit,
℟. Save us.

℣. Santisima Muerte, purifier of the nations,
℟. Save us.

℣. Divine Santisima Muerte, peace of the world,
℟. Save us.

℣. Divine Santisima Muerte, light of heaven and earth,
℟. Save us.

℣. Divine Santisima Muerte, rainbow of heaven,
℟. Save us.

℣. Santisima Muerte, hope of innocent children,

℟. Save us.

℣. Santisima Muerte, world of God,

℟. Save us.

℣. Santisima Muerte, Divine Wisdom,

℟. Save us.

℣. Divine Santisima Muerte, foundation of the world,

℟. Save us.

℣. O Most Precious and Divine Santisima Muerte,

℟. Cleanse the sins of the world.

℣. O Most Precious and Divine Santisima Muerte,

℟. Refine the world.

℣. O Most Precious and Divine Santisima Muerte,

℟. Teach us how to comfort, and to be grateful to God.

℣. Let us pray. O Most Precious and Divine Santisima Muerte, We put our faith, hope, and trust in Thee. Free all those who are in the hands of the infernal spirits, we beseech Thee. Protect the dying from the work of evil spirits, and welcome them into eternal glory. Have mercy on the world and strengthen it to praise and bless our Almighty Lord. We adore Thee, O Most Precious and Santisima Muerte, full of mercy. Amen.

℣. O Most Precious and Divine Santisima Muerte, heal the world of all misery and wickedness.

℟. O Most Precious and Divine Santisima Muerte, heal the world of all misery and wickedness.

℣. O Most Precious and Divine Santisima Muerte, heal the world of all misery and wickedness.

℣. Lord have mercy upon us.

℟. Lord have mercy upon us.

℣. Santisima Muerte, have mercy upon us.

℟. Santisima Muerte, have mercy upon us.

℣. Lord have mercy upon us.

℟. Lord have mercy upon us.

THE ROSARY OF SANTA MUERTE

The Santa Muerte Rosary, particularly with the Mysteries included, is a fairly new addition to Her cultus, however it is a powerful prayer for both devotional and magical purposes. Some devotees prefer to include the Mysteries for their devotional practices, so as to be able to meditate upon the powers given to the Most Holy Death by God. These Mysteries are sometimes omitted when using the Rosary magically, especially when doing group spell work. In this case, rather than meditating upon each Mystery as the prayers are recited, the devotee(s) meditate on their magical intent. There are many forms of the Rosary circulating out there, and what follows is but one version. There are also some additional prayers which may be included either before or after the Rosary, but perhaps the best prayer to include is the Litany after the Rosary is finished.

How to Pray the Rosary

Begin with the **Persinada**, and on the cross recite the **Opening Prayer** and **the Apostles' Creed**.

On the first large bead, pray the **Our Father**.

On the three smaller beads, pray the **Hail Mary**.

On the first large bead, announce the **First Mystery** (optional in group prayer and/or magical purposes), followed by one **Our Father**, one **Hail Mary**, and one **Glory Be**.

Pray the **Santa Muerte Prayer** on each of the 10 beads that follow. Conclude with a **Glory Be** and **Beloved Mother Death**.

On the second large bead, announce the **Second Mystery** (optional), and pray an **Our Father**, **Hail Mary**, and **Glory Be**. Continue in the same manner as above around the Rosary for each of the Mysteries.

On the center piece, pray the **Concluding Prayer**, followed by any other prayers you may desire, such as **the Litany**.

Finish with **the Sign of the Cross**.

The Mysteries of the Rosary

    1.   The Most Holy Death receives Her scythe, that by

its majestic delivery into Her right hand through our Lord God, the Father Almighty, She clears our path in life and severs earthly ties at the hour of death.

2. The Most Holy Death receives her cloak, with which she covers and protects the world.

3. The Most Holy Death receives the scales of justice, which she uses to restore balance and tranquility to the world.

4. The feet of the Most Holy Death are placed upon the earth that She may serve those who love Her.

5. The Most Holy Death is given the power to walk beyond the veil and back, to collect a soul when the flame of life is extinguished. O Most Holy Death, join us before the most high and bless us.

The Prayers of the Rosary

Persinada

+ By the Sign of the Holy Cross, + deliver us from our enemies, + O Lord our God, through the intercession of the Most Holy Death: In the name of the ✝ Father, and of the Son, and of the Holy Spirit. Amen.

Opening Prayer

O Most Holy Death, fill the hearts of your faithful and enkindle in them the fire of your love. Send forth your spirit to renew the face of the earth.

Let us pray. O Lord, who teaches the hearts of the faithful through the Most Holy Death, grant that, by means of the power of the Blessed and Divine Death Herself, we always receive wise counsel and ever rejoice in Her consolation. May the most precious Holy Death arise from Her kingdom, the Temple of Divine Wisdom, Tabernacle of Divine Knowledge, and Light of the Earth: Cover us with Your mantle now and forever. Amen.

Apostles' Creed

I believe in God, the Father almighty, maker of heaven and earth. I believe in Jesus Christ, His only Son, our Lord, who was conceived by the Holy Spirit, born of the Virgin Mary, suffered under Pontius Pilate, was crucified, died, and was buried; He descended into hell; on the third day He rose again from the dead; He ascended into heaven, he is seated at the right hand of the Father Almighty, He will come to judge the living and the dead. I believe in the Holy Spirit, the holy catholic Church, the communion of saints, the forgiveness of sins, the resurrection of the body, and the life everlasting. Amen.

Our Father

Our Father, who art in heaven, hallowed be Thy name. Thy kingdom come, Thy will be done on earth as it is in heaven. Give us this day our daily bread, and forgive us our trespasses as we forgive those who trespass against us. And lead us not into temptation; but deliver us from evil. Amen.

Glory Be

Glory be to the Father, and to the Son, and to the Holy Spirit; as it was in the beginning, is now, and ever shall be, world without end. Amen.

Hail Mary

Hail Mary, full of grace, the Lord is with thee. Blessed art thou amongst women, and blessed is the fruit of thy womb, Jesus. Holy Mary, Mother of God, pray for us sinners, now, and at the hour of our death. Amen.

Santa Muerte Prayer

My holy and beloved Mother Death, blessed are you amongst all beings and blessed is the time of my communion with you. Beloved Mother Death, intercede for us your children, now and at the hour of our death. Amen.

Beloved Mother Death

Beloved Mother Death, in life and in death, support us on our path. Most Holy Death, defend us from our enemies, and protect us now and at the hour of our death. Amen.

Concluding Prayer

Hail Holy Empress of the Underworld, Most Holy Death, have mercy on me. To you do I turn to in my times of need. Turn then, most gracious advocate, your eyes of mercy toward me. O Most Holy Death, use your powers on my behalf. Never forsake me, O Blessed Mother of all. Amen.

Additional Prayers (Optional)

Prayer to St. Michael

St. Michael the Archangel, defend us in battle. Be our defense against the wickedness and snares of the Devil. May God rebuke him, we humbly pray, and do thou, O Prince of the heavenly hosts, by the power of God, thrust into hell Satan, and all evil spirits, who prowl about the world seeking the ruin of souls. Amen.

An Act of Contrition

Holy Death, Queen of Heaven and Earth: forgive me, Mother, for being weak in my heart, mind, body, and soul. Wash away any evil I may have done, and purify my soul, so that it is so pure that I can stand before You without shame. Most Holy Death, I bring all my concerns to You, and I ask You with all my heart to look down upon me with pity, and forgive me if I have broken any promise to You. I need You in my life, guiding my every step with Your lamp, protecting me from those wishing my downfall, and keeping me safe from all harm and danger. Look down upon me, and smile upon me once more. Forgive my faults and weakness, for without You, I am lost in the darkness of this world. Amen.

Prayer for the Dead

Eternal rest grant unto them, O Lord, and may light perpetual shine upon them. May they rest in peace. Amen.

Prayer for Forgotten Souls

O merciful God, through the intercession of the Most Holy Death, take pity on those souls who have no particular friends and intercessors to recommend them to Thee, who, either through negligence or through length of time are forgotten by their friends and by all. Remember them, O Lord, and remember Thine own mercy, when others forget to appeal to it. Let not one soul ever be parted from Thee; may they rest in peace, and may light perpetual shine upon them. Amen.

DIVINATION WITH SANTA MUERTE

DEDICATING DIVINING TOOLS TO SANTA MUERTE

Any tool used for divining the past, present, and future can be dedicated to Santa Muerte so that only she will guide you through use and meaning. Through the dedication other outside spirits or influences will not be able to come through to interfere.

Santa Muerte since she is a complete and total magical system in herself, she also offers guidance in divination of any kind. She can teach the skills, she can strengthen the skills, and she can offer her guidance through any form of divination to those who ask.

Many people feel that her teachings are exceptional and easily learned. She can teach the skills of tarot, Spanish cards, pendulums, shells, dominos, scrying, dowsing rods, divination by smoke or flames, astrology, clairaudience, clairvoyance, numerology, palmistry, psychometry, and tasseography (tea leaf reading).

When it comes to divining with Santa Muerte her color is yellow. A yellow candle should be lit in order to gain insight and/or knowledge and should be lit during all readings. For this purpose you don't need to light a brand new yellow candle each time you do a reading, you can just use a plain seven day glass encased candle and use it over and over again.

Just as water is to always be present on her altar, a clear glass of water is also always placed on the table used for a reading. The water and candle can be placed anywhere on the table or location where the reading will be given. The presence of the water will make spiritual guidance flow freely and smoothly.

To dedicate a divining tools to Santa Muerte take the divining tool in your dominate hand (the one you write with) and offer it up to Santa Muerte's image while reciting the following prayer....

Santa Muerte, I open myself to your spiritual guidance
And consecrate these cards (or other divining tool) in your name (make the sign of the cross over the cards)
Guide me in their meaning and the story they hold
Light my way to the past, present, and future
Of all those that I seek clarity on
As you as my spiritual guide
Do not allow other spirits to interfere
You and you only Santa Muerte
Will guide me. Amen
(make the sign of the cross over the cards again)

Loteria Cards

1. El Gallo
"El que le canto a San Pedro no le volvera a cantar"
  The Rooster: He that sang for St. Peter will not return to sing again.
  One Word: Betrayal
  Interpretations: Beware of betrayal OR Someone who has betrayed you will not do it again OR The   person who is trying to warn/advise you is going to give up.

2. El Diablito
"Portate bien cuatito si note lleva el coloradito"
The Little Devil: Behave yourself so that the little red one doesn't carry you off.
One Word: Trouble
Interpretations: Make sure you are behaving yourself OR A little mischief is in the making OR someone is causing a bit of trouble in this situation.

3. La Dama
"La dama puliendo el paso, por todo la calle real"
The Lady: The lady taking an elegant walk along main street.
One Word: Grace
Interpretations: Handle this issue with grace and elegance OR Keep your manners about you OR This is all for show. Someone is showing off or pretending.

4. El Catrin
"Don ferruco en las almeda su baston queria tirar"
The Dandy: He wanted to toss away his cane and polish his steps.
One Word: Mastery
Interpretations: Let go of what you are holding onto and reach a new level OR Always strive for self -improvement

OR When something isn't working, try a new approach OR Be carefree, trust your instincts.

5. El Paraguas
"Para el sol y para el agua"
The Umbrella: For the sun and the rain
One Word: Protection
Interpretations: Someone or something is protecting you in good or bad times OR Be prepared for the good and the bad in any situation OR Always look at both sides of the situation (at least you have an umbrella)

6. La Sirena
"Con los cantos de sirena no te vayas marear"
The Mermaid: Don't go dizzy with the siren songs.
One Word: Mesmerize
Interpretations: Don't get carried away with emotion. OR Keep a clear head OR Look at the factors that are influencing you closely.

7. La Escalera
"Subeme paso apasito. Ho quieras pegar brinquitos"
The Ladder: Climb me step by step. You don't want to hop up.
One Word: Steady
Interpretations: Take it slow and steady, don't go too fast OR You are moving forward in the issue, keep going

8. La Bottella
"La hermienta del borracho"
The Bottle: The tool of the drunk
One Word: Obsession
Interpretations: Caution, there is an obsession or addiction here OR drinking is involved in this issue OR Someone is trying to forget their sorrow.

9. El Barril
"Tanto bebio el albanil que quedo commo barril."
The Barrel: The bricklayer drank so much that he ended up like a barrel.
One Word: Consequences
Interpretations: Beware of alcohol involved in this situation OR Do not over indulge in anything. OR There are always consequences for our actions. Examine what they might be. OR Too much of anything is not a good thing.

10. El Arbol
"El que a buen arbol se arrima buena sombra le cobija."
The Tree: He that seeks the shelter of a good tree, good shade covers him.
One Word: Positive
Interpretations: Good friends are like a good tree, they offer you shade OR Make good choices and you will be fine OR See the good in life and you will always be ok OR Make sure you are a person of character and you will be protected OR If you ask for help from a good person, you shall receive it.

11. El Melon
"Me lo das me lo quitas."
The Melon: Give it to me or take it from me.
One Word: Options
Interpretations: Simply take it or leave it, but make a decision. OR I care little which you do, just do it. OR Whichever choice you make, it won't have a big impact.

12. El Valiente
"Por que le corres cobarde trayendo tan buen punal."
The Hero: Why are you running like a coward when you are carrying such a good dagger?
One Word: Fear

Interpretations: Do not be afraid, you have what you need to be successful. OR Don't let fear rule this situation.

13. El Gorrito

"Ponle su gorrito al nene no se nos vaya a resfriar."

The Little Bonnet: Put the baby's little cap on, don't cause him to catch cold.

One Word: Caution

Interpretations: Someone needs protected or shielded in this issue OR Take care of those you care about

14. La Muerte

"La muerte sirqui siaca. La muerte tilica y flaca"

Death: Skinny death. The sycachi death, The tilica and skinny death.

One Word: Death

Interpretations: Denying yourself something, Dissatisfaction with body/self, Lovesick or missing someone OR an ending.

15. La Pera

"El que espera desespera."

The Pear: The one who waits despairs.

One Word: Procrastination

Interpretations: Do not wait too long or you will despair OR someone is giving up in this situation OR waiting is not the best choice here...take action.

16. La Bandera

"Verde blanco y colorado, ta badnera del soldado."

The Flag: Green, white, and red, the flag of the soldier

One Word: Defend

Interpretations: Stand behind what you believe in OR There are strong beliefs in this situation and people will defend their position.

17. El Bandolon

"Tocando su bandolon esta el mariachi Simon."

The Bandolon: There playing his bandolon is the mariachi Simon.

One Word: Dance

Interpretations: Someone is playing music in this situation (making others dance). OR Keep cheerful, follow the beat.

18. El Violoncello

"Creciendo se fue hasta el Cielo y como no fue violon. Tuvo que ser violocello"

The Cello: Growing, he went up to heaven and because he wasn't a violin, he had to be a cello.

One Word: Acceptance

Interpretations: Grow up and recognize the harsh realities of life OR When something blocks your way, go another direction OR Even if you can't have what you want, you can enjoy what you have.

19. La Garza

"Al otro lado del rio, tengo me banco de arena, donde se sienta me chata pico de garza moreno."

The Heron: On the other side of the river is the sandbar where sits my honey with a beak like a brown heron.

One Word: Seek

Interpretations: True love is available but it might take time to find it. OR Look and you will find what you are seeking, maybe in an unlikely place.

20. El Pajaro

"Tu me traces a puros brincos como pajaro en la rama"

The Bird: You've got me jumping to it like a bird on a branch.

One Word: Nervous

Interpretations: Someone/something is pulling your chain or making you jumpy. OR Don't just pretend to take action and flutter around...actually DO something about this issue. OR a certain level of nervousness is present.

21. La Mano

"La mano de un criminales" OR "La mano de un escribano"
The Hand: The hand of a criminal OR The hand of a scribe
One Word: Dishonesty
Interpretations: Someone in the issue is being dishonest OR People do not change their true nature. OR Be careful of the choices you make. OR Someone is keeping track of what is happening in this situation. There may be written evidence.

22. La Bota

"Una bota igual a la otra, Botala si no te sirve."
The Boot: One boot is the same as the other. Throw it away if you don't need it.
One Word: Similar
Interpretations: Of two choices, one is as good as the other OR Nothing has changed, things are in a rut OR You might "see" things differently but you are more alike than you think. OR Let go of things that no longer serve you.

23. La Luna

"El farol de enamorados"
The Moon: The lantern of lovers
One Word: Love
Interpretations: Love or romance is present OR Be careful that strong emotion is not influencing the situation OR Put a brighter light on the situation, something is clouding your vision.

24. El Cotorro

"Cotorro, cotorro, saca la pata y empiezame a platicar.""
The Parrot: Parrot, come out and start talking to me.
One Word: Communication
Interpretations: Someone needs to talk to you or you need to talk to someone. OR Don't get so busy that you do not listen to others. OR someone is gossiping or repeating what you say (caution)

25. El Borracho
"A ue borracho tan necio ya no lo puedo aguantar"
The Drunk: I cannot put up with the foolish drunk.
One Word: Foolish
Interpretations: Someone is being foolish in their ways or drinking too much. OR Be cautious about overindulgence of any kind. OR Remember what your actions look like to others.

26. El Negrito
"El que se comio el azucar"
The Negro: He who ate the sugar.
One Word: Resilient
Interpretations: Someone is experiencing difficulty but is still seeing the sweetness of life OR We do what we need to do to get through life.

27. El Corazon
"No me extranes corazon que regresso en el camion"
The Heart: Don't miss me, heart, because I will return in a truck.
One Word: Hope
Interpretations: Don't give up OR This love is true OR A longing for someone or something.

28. La Sandia

"La barriga que Juan tenia ere empacho de sandia."

The Watermelon: John's belly was stuffed full of watermelon.

One Word: Indulgence

Interpretations: Things are going well. OR Indulge in the pleasures of life OR There is enough here, do not worry.

29. El Tambor

"No te arrugues cuero viejo que te quiero pa'tambor."

The Drum: Don't wrinkle old leather, because I want you for my drum.

One Word: Value

Interpretations: Someone wants you. OR There is value here. OR Things may not be as they appear.

30. El Camaron

"Camaron que se duerme se lo lleva al corriente"

The Shrimp: The shrimp that sleeps is carried by the current.

One Word: Control

Interpretations: He who hesitates is lost. OR Take some action or you will be pulled about by others. OR Take control of the situation. OR Being passive is not the best choice here.

31. Las Jaras

"Las jaras del indio Adan donde pegan dan."

The Arrows: The arrows of the Indian Adam where they are joined together.

One Word: Bound

Interpretations: Something is bound tightly, just as the arrows. This may be good or bad. OR The arrows are held tightly together (arrows weapons...so) the challenge in this situation is difficult, like a battle.

32. El Musico

"El musico trompa de hule, ya no me quiere tocar."
The Musician: The musician has oiled his horn; now he doesn't want to play for me.
One Word: Deception
Interpretations: Something you thought was going to happen is not going to. OR Someone is "acting" as if they are a certain way or going to help BUT they are deceiving you OR Sometimes we think/feel a certain way but then when the time comes, we change our minds. OR Someone is being stubborn.

33. La Arana

"Atarmatamela a palos no me la dejes Hegar"
The Spider: Stun it with blows; just don't let her get me.
One Word: Action
Interpretations: Someone means you harm, be careful. OR You need to act, don't wait because waiting will put you at risk. OR this situation/person requires swift decisive action.

34. El Soldado

"Uno, does y tres, el soldado p'al cuartel."
The Soldier: One. two, three, and the soldier goes to the barracks
One Word: Order
Interpretations: Doing things in an orderly fashion or following directions will be helpful. OR Someone in this situation is being rigid and following along without questioning. OR Sometimes doing what we know how to do is the only choice.

35. La Estrella

"La guia de los marineros." OR "La Estrella polar de norte"
The Star: The sailor's guide OR The polar star of the north.
One Word: Guidance

Interpretations: Something or someone will guide you. OR You are lost, look for guidance OR There is hope and help available, you just need to recognize it.

36. El Cazo

"El cazo que te hago es poco"
The Melting Pot: The attention I pay you is little.
One Word: Ignore
Interpretations: You are missing something important. Pay attention OR Don't let things get to you, ignore them. OR You are feeling ignored in this situation.

37. El Mundo

"Este mundo es una bola y nosotros un bolon"
The World: The world is a sphere and we a foundation.
One Word: Foundation
Interpretations: Everything in the world/situation is inter-related. OR You must be strong, the foundation of this situation. OR Look to the foundation or the beginning of this situation.

38. El Apache

"Ay chihuahua! Cuanto apache con pantalon y huarache?"
The Apache: Oh my goodness! How many thugs there are with trousers and sandals?
One Word: Problems
Interpretations: You are surrounded by danger or problems. OR There are people involved in this that cannot be trusted.

39. El Nopal

"Al que todos van a ver cuando tiene que comer."
The Cactus: To which all go to see when they have to eat.
One Word: Source
Interpretations: You know what you have to do to get what you need. OR There is a source of help for you.

40. El Alacran

"El que con la cola pica. Le dan una paliza."
The Scorpion: He that bites with his tail, get beaten."
One Word: Danger
Interpretations: Someone is about to stab you in the back/betray you OR There is danger about, caution OR Sarcasm doesn't pay.

41. La Rosa

"Rosa, Rosie Rosaura: Rosa ven que te quiero ahora."
The Rose: Rosita, they see that I want you now.
One Word: Desire
Interpretations: Someone in this situation desires something very much OR Someone is being transparent. OR What is wanted is in plain sight and cannot be ignore

42. La Calavera

"Al pasar por el panteon, me encontre una calavera (un calaveron)""
The Skull: While passing the graveyard I found a skull (massive skeleton).
One Word: Surprises
Interpretations: Something about this situation is not exactly unexpected but a bit of a shock none the less OR Don't be surprised to find something exactly where it should be. OR When you get too close, expect to find something you aren't really looking for.

43. La Campana

"La campana y tu debajo." OR "Tu con la campana y yo con tu hermana."
The Bell: The bell and you beneath it. OR You with the bell and I with your sister.
One Word: Dread

Interpretations: Something is hanging over your head OR you are dreading something OR Look what I have compared to you.

44. El Canarito

"Tanto va el cantaro al agua, hasta que se rompe." OR "Todo cabe es un jarrito, sabiendolo acomodar."
The Pitcher: So much goes to the water, until it breaks. OR Everything fits in a jar, knowing how to accommodate it."
One Word: Seek
Interpretations: Someone is seeking something. OR Someone is being very persistent or perhaps obsessive. OR You know where to go to get what you need. OR Someone is not going to give up. OR When you make the right choice, everything will fit perfectly, so choose wisely."

45. El Venado

"El venado no ve nada." OR "El que brinca los penascos."
The Deer: The deer doesn't see anything. OR He who jumps the cliffs.
One Word: Naive
Interpretations: Someone is ignoring something in this situation OR Someone is not telling you the truth. OR Don't be naïve. OR Think, just don't follow someone over the cliff.

46. El Sol

"La cobija de los pobres."
The Sun: The shelter of the poor. The blanket of the poor.
One Word: Shelter
Interpretations: No matter how bad the situation, there is shelter for you. OR Look on the bright side of things. OR There are some things no one owns nor can be taken from you.

47. La Corona

"El sombrero de los reyes."

The Crown: The hat of kings.

One Word: Important

Interpretations: Beware who/what wears the crown. OR There is someone or something very important in this situation. OR Examine the importance of what is happening in this situation.

48. La Chalupa

"Rema y rema va lupita, sentada en su chalupita"

Little Boat: Paddle and paddle goes Lupita, seated in her little boat.

One Word: Baby-steps

Interpretations: Small steps move you forward. OR Just because something seems insignificant doesn't mean it is.

49. El Pino

"Fresco, oloroso y en todo tiempo hermoso"

The Pine: Fresh, fragrant, and at all times beautiful.

One Word: Success

Interpretations: There will be a positive outcome in this situation. OR Look at the good things in this situation. OR Always keep your head about you, stay calm and beautiful in the face of everything.

50. El Pescado

"El que por la boca muere, aunque mudo fuere."

The Fish: The one who dies by its mouth, even if he were mute.

One Word: Silence

Interpretations: It is better to keep your mouth shut. OR Someone is about to speak out and this will cause trouble. OR There is much miscommunication in this situation. OR Sometimes keeping your mouth shut doesn't work.

51. La Palma

"Palmera sube a la palma y bajame un coco real"
The Palm Tree: Keeper of the palms, climb the palm tree and bring me down a magnificent coconut.
One Word: Completion
Interpretations: You will receive that which you desire. OR Someone is working hard to please you.

52. La Maceta

"El que nace pa'maceta no sale del corridor"
The Flowerpot: He who is born to be a flowerpot will never leave the corridor.
One Word: Stagnant
Interpretations: Some people/things never change. OR Someone is not willing to do anything different than what they always do. OR Some things are meant to be.

53. El Arpa

"L'arpa vieja de mi suegra ya no sirve pa'tocar"
The Harp: My mother in law's old harp is no longer of use to play
One Word: Antiquated
Interpretations: Old ways of doing things are no longer useful. OR Let go when the time is right. OR There is a time for everything.

54. La Rana

"Al ver a la verde rana que brinco pego tu hermana"
The Frog: What a jump your sister gave, as she saw the green frog.
One Word: Self-aware
Interpretations: Recognize the things that scare you and others. OR It is just a little thing, nothing to be scared of. OR Be aware of the little things happening in this situation.

OR you will be surprised by something.

READING EXAMPLES

The deck a "mere" bingo type card game common in Mexico is full of vivid images and riddles that evoke many meanings that are indicative of life. Sometimes I think of the riddles almost as little life lessons.

Take La Chalupa for instance...

(The Sloop, little boat) Rema y rema va lupita, sentada en su chalupita.
Paddle and paddle goes Lupita, seated in her little boat.

Interpretations: Small steps move you forward. OR Just because something seems insignificant doesn't mean it is.

Either of these interpretations can be broadened based on other cards surrounding this particular one.

If next to El Gallo (The Rooster) it would be that your small steps aren't going to get you where you want to go...(he who sings will not sing again)

If next to La Escalera (The Ladder) it would support the card and say...yes slow and steady with your little steps will get you where you want to go.

If next to El Melon (The Melon) it would indicate that it's time to make a choice....stop just floating along and DECIDE....

As you can see the more you work with the Mexican Loteria cards and their little riddles the more they fine tune themselves into a sweet little oracle. I must say I have such a connection to them thought that perhaps that is why the readings seem to flow so nicely!

SPANISH PLAYING CARDS

The Meanings of the Cards

Copas

Ace (As/La Copeta): The house and the home. Stability. Consolidation. The present and current events. Something from the past which is re-emerging.

Two (Dos): Lover or friend. Friendship. A relative.

Three (Tres): Pleasant surprise. Relationship or partnership between two people. Engagement or marriage proposal. Happy event.

Four (Cuatro): Conversations. Reach an agreement. Good comments.

Five (Cinco): Jealousy around you. Malice from someone. Greed.

Six (Seis): Love. Start of a love affair. Passion.

Seven (Siete): Joy. Happy events. Things work out well despite bad beginnings. Things work out after being at a standstill.

Ten (Sota): Dark-haired woman with a light complexion. Housewife. Mother. Good female friend. Artist.

Eleven (Caballo): Unstable person. Well-known man. Manufacturer. Womaniser.

Twelve (Rey): Dark-haired man with a light complexion. Intelligent responsible and serious man. Capable.

Oros

Ace (As/El Oro): Triumph. Success. Letter, phone call, email, fax. News.

Two (Dos): Obstacles, difficulties, postponements, delays.

Three (Tres): A short journey. Exit. Short trip. Visiting or visitors.

Four (Cuatro): Present or gift. Small amount of money. A small loan.

Five (Cinco): The workplace. A meeting place. Assembly

or meeting. Hotel. Hospital. Large building.

Six (Seis): Night. Negligence. Trivialities. Small problems.

Seven (Siete): A lot of money. Successful business. A deal with a rival. Gains. Small prosperity. Good health. A rise in luck. Things start to move after delays.

Ten (Sota): Blonde or grey-haired woman. Professional woman. Medical woman or lawyer. Nun. Businesswoman. A rich woman.

Eleven (Caballo) : Traveller. Somebody from afar. Good friend. Intelligent, confident man. The matter at hand.

Twelve (Rey): Blond or grey-haired man. Professional man. Medical man or lawyer. Priest. Businessman. A rich man.

Bastos

Ace (As/El Bastillo): Deceit. Lies. Bad faith. Intrigue. Death.

Two (Dos): A child. Ideas. Projects. Plans. Hopes.

Three (Tres): Magic. Packages. Suitcases. Workplace. Religion.

Four (Cuatro): Setbacks and disaster. Small misfortune. Discovery. Something unexpected.

Five (Cinco): Jealousy. Deception. Troubled times. Something illegal or dishonest. Corruption.

Six (Seis): Long or short voyage. General changes.

Seven (Siete): The countryside or the seaside. Small city or town. Agricultural matters.

Ten (Sota): Dark-complexioned/olive-skinned, dark-haired woman. Divorced woman. Responsible, educated woman.

Eleven (Caballo) : Spirituality. Somebody far away. An acquaintance who is not often seen.

Twelve (Rey): Dark-complexioned/olive-skinned, dark-haired man. Divorced man. Responsible, educated man.

Espadas

Ace (As/La Espadilla): Total security. No room for doubt.

The law. Justice. Victory.

Two (Dos): Legal documents. Inheritance. The formalities. Studies or apprenticeships. Documents.

Three (Tres): On the way. Leaving someone or something. Divorce. The end. Resolution.

Four (Cuatro): Laid up in bed. Small suffering. Someone or something nearby.

Five (Cinco): Loss. Harm. Difficulties. Intrigue. Swindling. Robbery. Theft. Malice.

Six (Seis): Worries. Anxieties. Insecurity. Nervousness. Doubts. Obsession. Insanity. Instability. Anguish.

Seven (Siete): Sorrow. Tears. Chagrin. Heartache. Anger. Arguments. Lawsuit. Dispute. Disagreements. Opposition.

Ten (Sota): Very dark-haired woman. Divorced woman. Strong-willed and determined woman. Sister or female relative.

Eleven (Caballo): Sociable man. Drinker. Husband. Visitor. The matter at hand.

Twelve (Rey): Very dark-haired man. Divorced man. Strong-willed or determined man. Brother or male relative.

THE SPREADS

Three Card Spread:

This spread gives a quick answer/overview to a single question/issue. Lay out three cards in a row from left to right.

1   2   3

The cards represent past (card 1), present (card 2) and future (card 3).

This spread can also be extended to a Nine Card Spread using three cards for the past (top row), three cards for the present (middle row) and three cards for the future (bottom row).

<pre>
        1   2   3

        4   5   6

        7   8   9
</pre>

The Horseshoe Spread:
This spread gives a more general overview of your life and uses 21 cards. Lay down seven groups of three cards in the shape of a horseshoe or arch. Each group covers a category. The seven categories are:
1 The past situation.
2 The present situation.
3 Developments in the near future.
4 What you don't expect.
5 People around you.
6 Obstacles and opposition.
7 The outcome.

The Gitana Spread:
From left to right, lay three rows of seven cards. The top row of seven cards represents the past. The middle row the present and the bottom row of seven cards the future. This 21 card spread demands great skill and is not to be attempted until you are very confident with the meanings of the cards and combining them into a meaningful narrative.

SPIRITUAL BATHS OF SANTA MUERTE

Spiritual baths are related to healing practices throughout the world. These baths strengthen our connection with nature. The Santa Muerte baths aide in strengthen our connection with Santa Muerte or to cast her blessings upon us.

These baths can be taken for inner guidance and to uplift the soul, even for those who do not hold any particular religious or spiritual beliefs. Depending on the spiritual bath taken these baths can help end bad luck, open the way for love, happiness, money, healing, remove obstacles, break witchcraft and just about any other situation a person may face. Remember Santa Muerte is a complete and total magical system within herself.

Spiritual bathing helps to remove negative energy from the physical, mental and spiritual bodies that is collected from day to day. The practice cleanses the body of unseen energies and harmful conditions and is also used to attract certain kinds of energies you want.

The Moon

Among other things, the different phases of the moon add extra power to your spiritual bathing experience. Each lunar cycle offers different benefits. If you are going to incorporate the lunar influences in your spiritual baths just remember that during the waning moon is good for when you want to "remove", "lessen", "repel" or send something "away".

During the waxing moon is good for when you want to

"draw", "attract", "bring", "increase", or make something "grow".

During the new moon is good for when you want to start something "new" such as renewing your faith or a project. This is also a good moon phase to "connect" with Santa Muerte.

There are numerous places on the web that give the current phase of the moon. There are also moon phase programs you can download for free that will tell you what phase the moon is currently in, when it will end and when a particular moon phase will happen... do some research...these free programs are easy to find.

The Bath Ritual

The Santa Muerte baths are prepared with a variety of materials depending on its purpose. Some baths may contain spiritual oils, herbs or flowers and other plants. Bath ingredients are chosen for their energies and their connection to Santa Muerte.

For instance, if the bath is intended to attract love you would choose an herb or oil with these same properties. If the goal is to protect you from witchcraft the herbs should be chosen for their ability to give protection. Look in the lesson sent out earlier which lists the herbs connected to Santa Muerte.

When using herbs in the bath they are usually made into a "spiritual liquid" in a non-drinkable tea form. After being strained the liquid is reserved and poured into the tub water. All spiritual baths should contain at least ½ cup of Holy Water.

Spiritual baths are taken in a specific manner and if necessary a certain number of baths may be needed to obtain the best results. The best time to take a spiritual bath is at the crack of dawn but if this is impossible the next best time for spiritual bathing is at sundown.

Numbers play an important role and are believed to generate extreme amounts of energy. If you would like to include the power of numbers in your spiritual bathing experience here are the rules to follow.

For Santa Muerte baths when the goal is to "attract", "draw", "increase", or to "bring" something to you the spiritual bath should be made of 7 ingredients, including the ½ cup of Holy Water.
First you should fill the tub with plain bath water and after it is full you will add your ingredients. Next you should swirl the water around 7 times with your dominate hand (the one you write with). Light two white candles in honor of Santa Muerte and arrange them near the tub on the floor so that when you get out you will have to walk between them.

The candles can be any candle you choose as long as they are white. The exception would be if you are burning a Santa Muerte candle encased in glass. In this case the wax color can be of any color that comes with her candle.

Get in the tub and immerse yourself in the water 7 times, including your head. Next, stand up and with your hands wipe the water upwards on your body from your feet to your head, do this 7
times. Sit back down in the water and recite your prayers 7 times while you are soaking. You will take this same bath, in the same manner, for 7 consecutive days. After each bath you should save some of the bath water in a small container and add it to the next bath. Get out of the tub and walk in between the two Santa Muerte candles.

Get dressed in freshly laundered cloths, do not put on

clothing that has been previously worn even for a minute, they have to be freshly laundered. Do not towel dry, instead allow your body to air dry naturally. You can use a towel on your hair so that it isn't dripping wet. Pinch out the Santa Muerte candles, do not blow them out, and relight them the next day for your next bath.

At the last day of spiritual bathing allow the Santa Muerte candles to burn out completely.

Before allowing all of the water to drain out of the tub, take two small bowls of the bath water.

One bowl you will pour on the ground outside your home. The other bowl you will set upon the Santa Muerte altar so that she can further the blessing. This is the water you will add to your next bath. It remains on her altar overnight.

When the goal is to "control", "command", "dominate", or to "influence" something the spiritual bath should be taken the same as outlines above except you would replace everything with 9

instead of 7.

When the goal is to "remove", "lessen", "shrink", "rid" or "send away" (including breaking witchcraft) something the spiritual bath should be taken in the outline as above but replace

everything with 13. The only changes made for removing something is that you would wipe your body downwards instead of upwards.

And for just refreshing yourself spiritually take the above bath doing everything only once. You do not have to incorporate the magic of numbers into your Santa Muerte baths, they still work regardless. Numbers are only to add a little extra energy to your bathing experience.

After selecting the herbs you want to include in your bath

they must be made into tea form (non-drinkable) which I call "spiritual liquid". This is easily achieved by bringing 3 cups of water to a boil. Remove from heat and add your herbs. Cover and allow the liquid to steep for about 30 minutes. Strain out the herbs and use the liquid for the bath. The amount of herb you use is small. Just enough of each herb to fit into the center palm of your hand, not heaping. This would be close to about 2 tablespoons of each.

Burning incense during your ritual bath can an added advantage by bringing in helpful influences from the chosen fragrance and it adds to the focus of the bath itself. If you choose to burn incense during your bath select one that is pleasing to you since this will help you to relax and focus on the experience. Never burn an incense fragrance that you are not fond of, it will make your mind wander and cause unneeded distractions. They incense should always be calming, meditative and pleasing to your own personal likes.

SANTA MUERTE BATH MIXTURES

SANTA MUERTE BANISHING BATH
½ cup Holy Water
¼ cup sea salt
Hyssop
Basil

SANTA MUERTE LOVE BATH
½ cup Holy Water
Rosemary
Mint
Rose petals

SANTA MUERTE ABUNDANCE BATH
½ Cup Holy Water

Oregano
Pineapple Chunks
Yerba Santa

SANTA MUERTE BUSINESS SUCCESS BATH
½ Cup Holy Water
Rue
Allspice
Fennel

SANTA MUERTE LUSTFUL BATH
½ Cup Holy Water
Poppy Seed
Vanilla bean

SANTA MUERTE HEALING BATH
½ Cup Holy Water
Milk Thistle
Gardenia
Geranium

SANTA MUERTE ANTI WITCHCRAFT BATH
½ Cup Holy Water
Basil
Rosemary
Rue

SANTA MUERTE MONEY BATH
½ Cup Holy Water
Basil
Ginger
Lavender

SANTA MUERTE PROTECTION BATH

½ Cup Holy Water
Cumin
Bergamot
Float 3 pieces of aloe vera roots in the tub (Santa Muerte's herb of choice)

SPELLS OF SANTA MUERTE

La Tributa (The Tribute)

An important practice for La Santisima Muerte is La Tributa, the tribute. The purpose of la tributa is to gain the attention of La Muerte for a specific purpose or working, as well as to provide her with an offering at the threshold of her home, the cemetery. This should be done when you begin with Santisima, especially if you wish to know if she will assist you in spiritual workings rather than simply accepting you as a devotee.

Obtain an unglazed earthenware vase or pot. If the only thing you can find is a planter, then seal the bottom drain hole as it needs to hold water. At least a day before you perform the ceremony of la tributa paint a white skull on the vase/pot and let it dry. You'll also need six white roses, seven dimes, water, holy water, and siete machos cologne. Remove any thorns and leaves from the roses.

When it's time, gather everything together in front of your Santisima altar. Say the opening prayers, including asking God's permission to call upon La Muerte. Talk to La Madrina as you place the roses into the vase/pot, add the water, add three drops of holy water ("In the name of the Father, the Son, and the Holy Spirit"), sprinkle in some siete machos, and add the seven dimes. When this is complete, tell Santisima that you are leaving to take her tributa to her home and to meet you there to receive it. Close with three Our Fathers, and then immediately take the tributa to a cemetery and place it in the gateway, neither completely inside the cemetery nor out of it. Talk to Santisima about the reason you're doing this, and when you're finished thank her, stand up, turn and leave, but do not look back.

If you give her a tributa asking for her help, make sure that when she does it you give her a manda as payment, along with anything else you may have promised her.

SANTA MUERTE EMPLOYMENT SPELL

You will need:
3 white free standing candles
3 candle holders
Employment oil
1 white dressmakers pin (the ones with the colored ball on the top) Arrowroot
Paper
Pen
4 quarters

Directions:
If you know the name of the company you are going to apply to write it out on a blank piece of paper and set it aside for now. The three candles should be set up to form a sort of triangle pattern in front of the Santa Muerte statue. One directly in front of her and the other two towards the left and right of her image.

With the dressmakers pin carve the name of the place you are going to apply to and right below that carve Santa Muerte's name under it and your name under Santa Muerte's name.

Dress the three candles with employment oil and roll them in the arrowroot. Place the candle in their holders. The paper that you wrote the name of the company on goes under the candle holder that is directly in front of Santa Muerte.

Light the one single candle that is directly in front of Santa

Muerte and recite the opening prayers through the Invocation

Now light the candle to the left and recite the following prayer...

Santa Muerte, I ask for your blessings
To increase and better my finances
Help me to overcome all my debts
And to meet my household bills
Help me to have the means to feed my family
To cloth them and to provide medical needs
Relieve me of the pressure of financial difficulties
And grant us with enough left over
to enjoy the pleasures and luxuries in life. Amen

Now light the candle to the right and recite the following prayer...

Santa Muerte, bless these candles
so that they are empowered with your strength
I ask that you grant me the position I am about to apply for
through (name the company)
remove any obstacles that may prevent me from getting this job and take over the mind of the person who makes this decision
let him/her look with great interest on my application

Place one quarter on each of the candle holders, even if you have to balance them up against it, and place the fourth quarter in Santa Muerte's hand (you can tape it there if need be). Allow the candles to burn for 1 hour each day until they are consumed.

SANTA MUERTE HEALING SPELL

This is a take on my St Camillus healing box. Actually, it will work for any Saint or deity you choose to work with, just change the name accordingly. Here we will use it with Santa Muerte.

This box can be created to offer healing energy to those in need. This is a simple concept which is strengthened with the help of Santa Muerte. For this spiritual work you will need a small wooden box. I don't believe in using plastic in spiritual practices and find that wood brings strength and an added element to the work at hand. If you cannot find a wooden box the next best thing would be cardboard or paper mache (but wood is the absolute best).

The box can be left simple or you could decorate it in any way you like. I know many people who decorate these healing boxes with glitter, sequins, pictures, written prayers, or shells. As for myself I like to decorate the outside with the Golden Mean Spiral since this spiral in sacred geometry contains much healing abilities. The Golden Mean Spiral is found throughout life and is very powerful. You may even choose to decorate it with small printed photos of Santa Muerte.

Once you have the box decorated the way you want it, the bottom inside of the box should be fitted with a piece of blue felt cut to size. Inside, under the lid, a small mirror should be glued
with the mirror facing the inside when the lid is closed. This magnifies and keeps the healing energy inside. You can purchase small cut mirrors at any craft store for about 50 cents.

Next, light a candle to Santa Muerte and ask for the box to contain her essence, love, and strength for the purpose of healing those in need. While the candle burns the box is left to the right of the candle, yet away from the heat of it and should remain there until the candle is consumed.

Once the candle goes out, place a prayer card or a printed image of Santa Muerte inside the box which was previously sprayed lightly with Holy Water. This should remain inside the box at all times. You can also place other items inside to further add healing strength such as a clear quartz crystal which is known for its magnification properties.

To the box you can then add hand written names or photos of those who need healing. The names or photos are kept inside the box until relief from their illness is granted. Once granted, the name or photo of the person is left on the grounds of the church. Some people like to burn the names or photos but I feel that burning an image or the representation of a person is too harsh. Leaving them in the church seems to me the proper way to go.

Once a week you offer Santa Muerte prayer asking for her intersession in healing and the outside of the box is lightly misted with Holy Water. This is a very good way of sending healing to anyone in need and is powerful in absent healing.

Santa Muerte Prayer for Healing
Santa Muerte, compassionate and powerful lady
You have the power to heal those who are ill
And free them from their suffering
I ask you to look with favor
On those names contained within this box
Those who are weak
Come to the assistance of these people
Who are afflicted with illness
Obtain for them health in mind and body.
Amen.

SANTA MUERTE LOVE SPELL
This is the traditional and complete Santa Muerte love spell. Before doing this love spell, or any other spell, make sure to go through the proper protection that you would normally

use.

You will need:
Aloe vera plant
2 lengths of Red ribbon
Vase of tap water
Six white flowers (any kind)
Photo of the target person
Photo of yourself
3 red dressmakers pins (the ones with the colored ball on the top) Small amount of red fabric
Red free standing candle
Candle holder
Red votive candles
Siete Machos cologne
Glass of water

Directions:
Get a clear glass of water and add to it nine drops of Siete Machos cologne. Santa Muerte likes this fragrance. Place this on her altar. Get a new aloe vera plant, not the one you would normally have hanging on the altar. This one will be for the purpose of the love spell alone. Tie the root end with a length of red ribbon, red string, or red yarn and hang it upside down over the altar. For this love spell you can also suspend it from Santa Muerte's hand.

Fill a vase with fresh tap water to the top and place the six white flowers inside. This vase is then taken to the cemetery. Set the vase either at the gate of the cemetery or on the first grave you see as you walk inside. Kneel and concentrate on the purpose of the spell. When you're done leave the vase there and return to your altar. After leaving the cemetery you should not stop off to run errands or visit with friends but go immediately back to your altar.

Take the photo of the target person (the one you are doing

134

the work on) and the photo of yourself and pin them together, face to face, with the red dressmakers pin. The other pin is stuck through the photos to form the shape of the cross.

Place the pinned photos in the red fabric and roll it shut and secure it with a red ribbon. This goes under your bed.

Light the red votive candle. This candle should constantly be lit during the entire time of the spellwork. When the red votive is about to go out make sure to light another candle in its place.
Place the red free standing candle in the candle holder. Then recite the following prayer.....In the prayer when you come to the spot where it mentions "driving the needle into a candle" you are going to take the third red dressmakers pin and stick it in the candle and then light it. The red votives are for Santa Muerte. The red free standing candle is the one that is part of the spellwork. The free standing candle is put out and re-lit after each session of the spell.

The best time to perform each session of the spell is late in the night when you think the person will be asleep. This spell should be performed for the length of 48 days no matter if you have already received the desired outcome.

Prayer of the Santa Muerte
Jesus Christ the conqueror, who on the cross was conquered, conquer (name of person), that he be conquered with me in the name of the Lord
if you are a fierce animal tame as a lamb,
tame as the flower of rosemary; you must come;
you ate bread, of him you gave me
and through the most strong word that you gave me,
I ask that you bring me (name of person),
that he be humbled, defeated at my feet
to complete what to me he has offered.
Santisima Muerte, I beseech you

inasmuch as Immortal God formed you
with your great power over all mortals
so that you might place them in the celestial sphere
where we may enjoy a glorious day without night
for all eternity and in the name of the Father,
the Son and the Holy Spirit,
I pray and I beseech you
that you be my protectress
and that you concede all the favors that I ask of you
until the last day, hour and moment
in which your Divine Majesty commands
to take me before your presence. Amen.

JACULATORIA

Santa Muerte, do not leave me without protection.
do not allow (name of person) one moment of tranquility;
bother him every moment, mortify him and disturb him
so that he always thinks of me.
(pray 3 Our Fathers)

PRAYER TO ATTRACT THE SPIRIT OF THE PERSON

Spirit, body and soul of (name of person)
come because I am calling you, I dominate you
tranquility you will not have
until you come surrendered at my feet.
As I pass this needle through the middle of this candle (stick
the pin in the candle) the thought of me will pass through
the middle of your heart
so that you will forget the woman you have and come when
I call you.
(repeat this 3 times)
Angel of your day, angel of today, Guardian Angel of (name
of person) bend the heart of (name of person) so that he
will forget the woman he has and come surrendered with
love to my feet.

PRAYER TO CALL THE GUARDIAN ANGEL OF.....

Holy Guardian Angel of (name of person)
do not allow him tranquility until he is at my side.
Saint, oh Saint of my name and devotion
That he be content with me is what matters to me.
Anima Sola, that he may love me, that I may love him,
return to me the affection of (name of person) who has gone.
Spirit, body, and soul of (name of person) from this moment
he will not have any joy, any desire other than that for me;
Spirit, body, and soul of (name of person) that his love, his affection, his fortune, his caresses, his kisses, everything of him be only for me.
Body and soul of (name of person) you may not go to see, not love no other woman other then me.
Spirit of San Cipriano, bring him to me
Spirit of Santa Elena, bring him to me
Spirit of Santa Marta, bring him to me
Spirit of La Caridad de Cobre, bring him to me.
Virgen de Covadonga, that you might bring me (name).
(repeat this 3 times)

Spirit of the light that illuminates the clouds of the souls
light the brain of (name of person) so that he remembers
me in all that he does, give this to me, impulsed through
your powers so that he be a slave to my love; tranquility give
him not until he is at my side.

PRAYER TO THE ALOE

Virtuous aloe, blessed aloe,
Holy aloe, sacred aloe,
through your virtue that you gave to the Apostles
I ask that you extend this virtue to me

because I venerate you and I love you
so that you may free me from evil acts,
sickness, bad luck, that my businesses do well,
in business transactions and that you drive evil away from
my home and free me from enemies everywhere I may go:
that you give me work, blessings, fortune and money
with ease and the least effort,
your virtue will make me strong, famous, fortunate and
joyous, do not place obstacles in what I am ambitious for,
desire or propose to do, make me a flattering success;
this divine virtue that God gave you,
in God I believe and in you I trust.
Through all of the virtues that you concede to me
I will defeat all of the obstacles that are presented to me
and my home will fill with blessings with your virtue
sublime and portentous Holy aloe.

SANTA MUERTE BREAKUP SPELL

This is used to split two people up

Needed:

1 fresh lemon
Bat blood oil
Black pepper
1 rusty nail
Cayenne pepper
9 black dressmakers pins (the ones with the colored balls on
the end) 1 yard of black fabric
Black yarn
9 black candles (free standing)
Dirty paper (go out and rub it all over the dirt if you have
to) Black ink pen
6 aspirin tablets
glass jar with a lid
white vinegar

Directions:

Dress the nine candles with the bat blood oil and the black

pepper. Rip two small pieces of the dirty paper. You want rough edges on the paper that's why you rip it instead of cutting it. In black ink, write the females name 9 times on one piece of the dirty paper and write the name of the male 9 times on the other piece of dirty paper. Write the names as small as you can and rip the paper around the names so that you can get the paper a small size.

You will light one candle every day for 9 days but you dress them all at once. Light one of the black candles. Cut the lemon in half. Pick up one half of the lemon and insert one of the name papers into one half of the lemon and the other name paper into the other half of the lemon. Push and manipulate the paper until it's inside the lemon and say...

I baptize you as (female's name) before the powerful image of Santa Muerte. From now on you will be known as (female's name).

Repeat this baptism with the other half of the lemon for the mans name.

Now with the females half of the lemon insert 3 aspirins into the pulp. As you do that say...
"(female's name), your relationship with (mans name) will sour, by the power of Santa Muerte.
Every time you are in his presence a repulsive sour taste will come into your mouth.

Repeat this process with the mans half of the lemon. This time say... (man's name), your relationship with (female's name) will sour, by the power of Santa Muerte. Every time you are in her presence a repulsive sour taste will come into your mouth.

Over each half of the lemon skin mark an invisible an X across the skin of the lemon using the thumb of your dominate hand and say...

I curse you and command you to break and end your relationship now, by the powerful scythe of Santa Muerte. Do this with both lemon halves.

Sprinkle each lemon half with cayenne pepper on all sides and say...

I curse you and command you break this relationship.

Put the two lemon halves back together with the rusty nail between them. And put the lemon back together with the pins, the pins should hold it together. As you insert the pins, curse the couple nine times by saying...

If you do not obey my command to breakup this relationship at once you will suffer in the fires of hell for eternity.

Then wrap the lemon in the black fabric and begin to bind it with the black yarn. As you wrap the lemon, tie the yarn in nine knots and place the lemon near the candle. For the next eight days repeat the curse you put on the couple. The one that states you'll burn in the fires of hell and tell them both that the only way to end their bad luck is to break up.

Each night place the remaining candle wax and any other remains of the ritual in a jar. After nine days, cut off the yarn and fabric from the lemon. Remove the nine pins and separate the lemon and bury the man's half of the lemon in the backyard where the sun does not shine, like under a bush. So you might want to get creative and find a way for you to identify who's half is who's.

With the girls half of the lemon place it in the jar with all the remains you have been collecting and fill the jar with vinegar. Wrap the jar in black fabric and tie it up with black yarn, making nine knots as before. Take the jar and dispose of it in a public dumpster. Call the girl by name and command her to leave. Walk away and don't look back.

SANTA MUERTE SPELL TO GET RID OF A TROUBLESOME NEIGHBOR

This is used to make a neighbor move

You will need:

2 black freestanding candles (one candle for the man and for the woman of the household.....if there is only one head of household you will only need 1 black candle) 2 candle holders

Get away oil

Cayenne pepper

1 black dressmakers pin (the ones with the colored ball on the end) Parchment paper

Black ink pen

Dirt from the neighbor's yard

Charcoal disk

Incense burner

Sea salt

1 small bowl

1 rusty nail

Asafetida

Wooden matches

Dirt from a dead plant

Vinegar

Directions:

Take the candles and with the black dressmakers pin carve the names of the neighbors on each of the candles. Write the woman's name one candle and the man's name on the other candle.

Pour a small amount of the vinegar into the bowl and add 2 large pinches of sea salt. Baptize each of the candles to each of the neighbors using the vinegar and salt mixture. This gives the candles a personal link to the neighbors and sours their desire to live in the house. This also works well for domination purposes.

Take the male candle in your left hand. With your right hand dip your fingers into the vinegar mixture and sprinkle it over the candle in the sign of the cross and say.....

"Before the altar of Santa Muerte I baptize you (man's name) in the name of the Father, and of the Son and of the Holy Ghost. From this moment on you are (man's name) and you will obey my every command."

Place his candle in a candle holder. Now take the woman's candle in your left hand. With your right hand dip your fingers into the vinegar mixture and sprinkle it over the candle in the sign of the cross and say.....

"Before the altar of Santa Muerte I baptize you (woman's name) in the name of the Father, and of the Son and of the Holy Ghost. From this moment on you are (woman's name) and you will obey my every command."

Place her candle in a candle holder. Pour a small amount of the get away oil on the palm of your dominate hand (the one you write with) and dress the male candle. Begin rubbing the oil on the candle from the bottom of the candle towards the top of the candle. Do not apply the oil from the top down. Since you want to "make" them move, dominate them, "bring" them ill wishes you dress the candle from the bottom towards the top. While you are applying the oil say.....

"(Man's name) you will relocate immediately or you will face serious setbacks, misfortunes and illness. To avoid this move now! I plant this seed within your mind and it will grow rapidly, worrying you and causing you unsettlement until you relocate."

Then to Santa Muerte say....
"Santa Muerte, go, go and visit them and cause them fear to remain in that house. Allow them to see you dearest Santa"

Now take some of the dirt you collected from the neighbor's yard and dress the male candle with it from the bottom to the top of the candle and say.....

"Leave now!"

Place his candle in the candle holder. Pour a small amount of the get away oil on the palm of your dominate hand and dress the female candle. Begin rubbing the oil on the candle from the bottom towards the top of the candle.
While you are applying the oil say.....

"(Woman's name) you will relocate immediately or you will face serious setbacks, misfortunes and illness. To avoid this move now! I plant this seed within your mind and it will grow rapidly, worrying you and causing you unsettlement until you relocate."

Then to Santa Muerte say....

"Santa Muerte, go, go and visit them and cause them fear to remain in that house. Allow them to see you dearest Santa"

Now take some of the dirt you collected from the neighbor's yard and dress the female candle with it from the bottom to the top of the candle and say.....

"Leave now!"

Place her candle in the candle holder.

With the rusty nail make a small hole on the side of each of the male and female candles. Be careful not to break the candle in half. When you are making the hole you will have to dig out small sections of the wax slowly in order to keep from cracking the wax. Go slow. Make the hole small but large enough to fit the rolled name paper inside. The hole does not have to be deep, just deep enough to hold the paper in place.

With the parchment paper and the black ink pen write the name of the man on the paper and sprinkle some cayenne pepper over the name. Roll the paper up tightly with the cayenne pepper inside and stick the roll into the hole in the man's candle. Do the same for the woman's candle.
Light both of the candles with the wooden matches and say.....

"I dominate you, I control you and I cause you to relocate immediately. Do not hesitate. Move now or suffer the consequences."

Place the charcoal disk in the incense burner and ignite it with a wooden match. When the coal is lit, place a large pinch of the asafetida in the center of the coal. When it begins to smoke take each of the candles and pass it over the smoke and say.....

"Leave now!"

Take a pinch of the dirt that you collected from the dead plant and slowly sprinkle it over the coal. Don't place too much on it or it will go out. Allow the coal to burn out. Do not place any more of the herb on it.

Burn the candles for 5 minutes every day until they completely burn out. Each time you light the candles you should talk to them. Tell them that they are to move immediately or they will certainly suffer the consequences.

Once more call on Santa Muerte and say.....
"Santa Muerte, go, go and visit them and cause them fear to remain in that house. Allow them to see you dearest Santa"

Once the candles have been used, collect all the remains (except the ash from the charcoal) in a bag and if you can, bury them in your neighbor's yard. If this is too difficult maybe there is a place somewhere in their yard that is overgrown that you can throw the remains in so that they won't be found.

If this is still too difficult take the candles and rub them on the tires of their cars so that some of the wax gets on the tires and throw the rest away in a public dumpster.

Collect the ash from the charcoal and scatter them in the neighbor's yard. Try to scatter some on their doorstep so that they have to walk through it. Also try to get some of the ash on the doorknob so that it will get on their hands. Scatter the rest in their yard.

SANTA MUERTE BUSINESS SUCCESS SPELL

Needed:
Dirt from the business location
1 small jar with a tight fitting lid
1 small image of Santa Muerte
7 coins
1 small magnet
Business success oil
1 green votive candle
1 candle holder
Dirt from 7 successful businesses
Brick dust (red)
Blue flag

Directions:
Note: You can do the preparation for this spell at home and then take the finished product to the business location. Place the green votive candle in the holder. Light it and dedicate it to Santa Muerte, invoking her help for this spell.

INVOCATION

Santisima Muerte, I invoke your presence here tonight (today). Join me here before the altar which I have erected in your name. Make your presence known to me. I ask for your guidance and your protection. Santisima Muerte, cast your strength upon me at this moment and in the way you see fit for me to feel your presence here, make me sensitive to it, make me aware Santa Muerte (concentrating), Santa Muerte (concentrating), Santa Muerte (concentrating), (clap loudly 3 times). (Make your request for her help in the spell).

Next take the empty jar and lid and dress the outside with the business success oil. Now place half of the dirt you collected from the locations of the seven successful businesses inside the jar.
Place the dirt from your business location inside and cover it with the remainder of the dirt from the seven successful businesses. You want to sandwich your dirt in between their dirt. Next pray the following...
"Santa Muerte, grant that my business is as successful as those who are placed within this container. Bring my business good luck, abundance, and prosperity."

Place the seven coins on top and pray...
"Santa Muerte, grant that my business is filled with money, riches, wealth, and customers."

Place the blue flag inside and pray....
"Santa Muerte, grant that my business is filled with customers who are happy and that they leave my business

with good things to say. Grant that they spread good words about my business."

Place the red brick dust inside and pray....
"Santa Muerte, allow that my business be prosperous. Give it a solid foundation and the strength to overcome and grow over any competition. "

Place the small magnet inside and pray...
"Santa Muerte, attract to my business good luck, riches, wealth, prosperity, repeat customers, and success."

Place the small image of Santa Muerte inside and pray...
"Santa Muerte, strengthen these intentions with your blessings. Amen."

Once a month dress the outside of the jar with the business success oil and pray...
"Santa Muerte, strengthen these intentions with your blessings. Amen."

SANTA MUERTE STOP GOSSIP SPELL

Needed:
Paper doll
Black thread
Brand new needle
1 black candle (any size)
Candle holder

Directions:
This spell is done through the use of a witness or proxy. Instead of ritually making a doll to represent the person spreading the gossip we are going to use a paper doll.. You

can use print these and use them as a representation of the person. Use the male doll to represent a man and the female doll for a woman.

Print the paper doll and cut it out. On the back of the paper doll write the persons full name and any other personal information you may have on the person such as birth date, age, nickname, etc. You can even color the doll to match it to the person (black, brown, blonde hair, moles, scars, skin tone, etc).

Now place the black candle in the holder and light it. Offer this candle to Santa Muerte and pray...
"Santa Muerte, intercede on my behalf. Grant me protection from those who talk bad about me.
Cast a shadow of darkness over this person who intends to harm me through words."

Take the needle and thread and begin sewing in a zigzag direction over the mouth of the paper doll and pray...
"Santa Muerte, as I sew shut the mouth of (name of person) I ask that you seal it closed forever.
When (name of person) thinks about talking badly about me tighten their mouth closed even tighter. Do not let the words escape from his/her lips."

Take another length of the black thread and tie it around the neck of the paper doll and suspend it anywhere on Santa Muerte's statue and pray...
"Santa Muerte, I place my enemy in your hands in order to control his/her actions. Intercede for me Santa Muerte and silence this person now."

Allow the candle to burn. Leave the doll hanging from the statue in order to control the situation. When you feel that the problem is solved and the person is no longer spreading gossip about you take the doll and burn it.

SANTA MUERTE COURT CASE SPELL
Needed:
1 handful of marigold flowers
3 brand new thin nails
Santa Muerte Oil
Court Case Oil
Holy Water
1 glass encased Santa Muerte candle
Parchment paper
Blue ink pen
1 small white plate
White cloth

Directions:
The first thing that should be done is the cleansing of the body. Take a bath or shower and put on fresh clean clothes. Once your body is clean of the day's dirt then you are ready to perform the ritual. Many people like to use a special bath additive to incorporate the act of bathing as part of the ritual itself. If this is the case, you can take about 2 cups of fresh rosemary and boil it in 2 cups of water. Strain and add the liquid to your bath water for spiritual cleansing.

Spread the white cloth on the floor or over Santa Muerte's altar. Any place is fine as long as the items won't be disturbed. Then place all the items on the white cloth.

Take the glass encased Santa Muerte candle and on the top of the wax carve the Star of David around the wick with one of the nails. While carving the Star of David around the wick, concentrate and recite the following prayer to Santa Muerte asking for her help in your victory.
Santa Muerte
I invoke your most powerful help
At this time that I find myself in need
With your protective scythe

Cut away any words, thoughts,
Evidence, witnesses, actions,
And sentences that may be
Directed towards me
Keep me safe from
Being found guilty
By any means
Silence those
Who may speak against me
Give the judge
Whomever it may be
The eagerness to
Turn a kind eye in my direction
Santa Muerte I make my plea before you
(make your special request)
Remove all people, places, and things
That may be a threat against me
Drive away any unseen misfortune
And protect my freedom Amen

Place 3 drops of the court case oil over the wax inside the Star of David and dress the outside of the glass encased candle with the Santa Muerte oil until it is well coated but not slippery. Make sure to coat the bottom of the glass as well.

Place the glass encased candle on the white plate and surround the bottom of the candle with the marigold flowers. Choose one of the triangles from the Star of David that you carved and stick one nail into each of the three points of the triangle. Light the candle to Santa Muerte. Sprinkle Holy Water over the rest of the items

On the parchment paper with the blue in pen write the outcome you want and place it under the plate the candle is on. Recite Psalm 7 and Psalm 35

DISPOSING OF USED RITUAL ITEMS

Once you have finished with a Santa Muerte spell it's important to remove the remains of any used items away of your immediate surroundings. Used items should be disposed of as soon as you are finished. Never allow these items to remain in the home longer than necessary.

Anything evil or harmful that was attracted during the ritual could leave a negative energy behind. Items that are not disposable such as a crucifix or another item you want to keep should be cleansed immediately and be made pure again.

These used items should never be handled by anyone other than yourself. Since you are the one who did the spellwork it is up to you to properly dispose of the remains.

To cleanse a tool that is not disposable you can wash the item with sea salt and Holy Water. Sea salt is one of the most widely used cleansing elements because it is simple and effective in removing all traces of evil and it is widely available. This can be done in two ways using the dry method or the wet method.

For the dry method just place the item in a bowl and cover it completely with sea salt. This is the least preferred method since it takes at least 24 hours to purify the item. The wet method works much faster and is the one most used since you are not left without a pure and cleansed tool.

Mix a small container with 1 cup filtered water and ¼ cup sea salt. Wet the item to be clean in the salty solution for five minutes. Rise with clear water and spray the entire object with Holy Water on all sides while saying.....

"In the name of Jesus Christ, all evil will leave from here"

Your item is ready to use again. Any time you cleanse an item with holy water you should always use the term..... "In the name of Jesus Christ" (or other deity you place your

faith in) Place all ritual remains in a plastic bag and tie it securely shut. Discard the bag in an outdoor trash container. Do not throw the bag away in the trash container that is located anywhere inside
your home. I like to take extra precautions and pour some salt over the items before I secure the bag. Salt is very purifying and protective.

Items that were used to BRING an energy to you should be collected in a bag or a small box and buried in your backyard. The only time it is acceptable for another person to touch the remains is when you have done spellwork for another person intended to BRING something towards them. In this case since the desired goal is for them they should take the remains and bury them in their own backyard.

For those who do not have a yard to bury these items you can fill a small terracotta plant container with soil and bury the remains in the pot. Afterwards, the pot should be left near the front door of their home. The buried item should remain in the container until the results are seen and for three weeks following. At that time the item can be taken out and discarded in a natural body of water such as your local lake, river or a nearby pond or in an empty field.

Items that were used for healing someone of an illness should be sprayed with Holy Water and placed in a plastic bag. The bag should be left on the grounds of a church which will bring a much stronger and faster healing.

Used candles can be discarded in an indoor trash container.

Holy items that are no longer useful should be left on the grounds of a catholic church.
Sometimes Saint Statues are known to break. This happens because the Saint has helped to keep someone safe, usually you. The amount of negativity encountered breaks or chips

the image.

When statues break or chip they are have served their purpose and should be disposed of. This goes for rosaries, holy medals, prayer cards and any other religious item that has served its purpose.

Ash from burnt herbs and incense should be wrapped in a clean paper towel and disposed of in a natural uninhibited area such as a park. Anyplace that is not occupied by traffic or homes are good places. These ashes should be placed on the earth and allowed to be carried away by the wind.

Bath water can be allowed to go down the drain but you should collect at least one small container and dispose of it outdoors (or a small amount saved and placed on the Santa Muerte altar for later use)

Any item used for the removal of witchcraft or spell breaking should be burned on an open fire outdoors. In today's world out bbq grills are the safest way of disposal. You can make a "bowl"
from aluminum foil and place the items inside so that all the ash is collected. Once the items are burnt close the foil bowl and dispose of it away from your property. Anything used for the removal of witchcraft or breaking a spell should never be discarded in any trash container on your property....inside or out.... always dispose of the remains in a public trash container OFF and AWAY from your home.

If when burning these items they explode or make strange noises such as shrieks or loud pitched sounds these are signs that the evil or spell was sent back to where it came from. It's a sign of separation from the person placed upon. Sometimes if you look into the fire as it burns you can see faces or symbols and other pictures.

After disposing ritual remains make sure to spray your

hands with Holy Water.

SANTA MUERTE RECIPES

SANTA MUERTE OIL RECIPES

BASES FOR MAKING ALL THE OILS LISTED BELOW

For either of the oils use extra virgin or virgin olive oil. Get a mortar and pestle or any other suitable container to grind herbs in and pour in about 1 ½ to 2 ounces of olive oil. Next add 3 tablespoons of the dry herb. Grind the herb into the oil in order to release its natural oil and fragrance. You want this incorporated into the olive oil. Once the herb is grinded transfer the olive oil with the crushed herb into a glass jar and cover it with a tight fitting lid. Leave the jar outdoors in the sun. If you wish you can also leave the jar on a sunny windowsill. Allow the jar to remain in a sunny location for 4 days. Then strain and save the oil in smaller bottles. If you prefer a more fragrant oil add more crush herb into the oil. To keep the oil from becoming stale you can either add a little benzoin or a crushed vitamin c tablet to the oil. If you add more than one herb make sure to increase the olive oil by 2 tablespoons.

SANTA MUERTE ALTAR OIL

2 ounces olive oil
2 tablespoons rue
1 cinnamon stick
9 drops myrrh oil

If you prefer a tinted oil try adding red, green, or yellow food coloring one drop at a time until you achieve the desired color. Other good additives to this oil would be clear quartz chips or plant stems/root.

SANTA MUERTE DRAWING OIL

2 ounces olive oil
9 drops lodestone oil
9 drops sandalwood oil
2 tablespoons chamomile or bayberry
If you prefer a tinted oil try adding green, or blue food coloring one drop at a time until you achieve the desired color. Other good additives to this oil would be lodestone chips or small magnet pieces.

SANTA MUERTE MONEY OIL

2 ounces olive oil
2 tablespoons bergamot
9 drops frankincense
If you prefer a tinted oil try adding green food coloring one drop at a time until you achieve the desired color. Other good additives to this oil would be shredded money.

SANTA MUERTE PEACEFUL HOME OIL

2 ounces olive oil
2 tablespoons rosemary
1 tablespoon verbena
9 drops sandalwood oil
If you prefer a tinted oil try adding blue food coloring one drop at a time until you achieve the desired color. Other good additives to this oil would be small amethyst chips.

SANTA MUERTE LOVE OIL

2 ounces olive oil
2 tablespoons yarrow
2 tablespoons yerba mate
9 drops rose oil
If you prefer a tinted oil try adding red food coloring one

drop at a time until you achieve the desired red or pink color. Other good additives to this oil would be small rose quartz chips, rosebush thorns.

SANTA MUERTE PROTECTION OIL

2 ounces olive oil
2 tablespoons cat's claw
1 tablespoon alum
9 drops cypress oil

If you prefer a tinted oil try adding blue food coloring one drop at a time until you achieve the desired color. Other good additives to this oil would be whole peppercorn, plant parts.

SANTA MUERTE HOUSE BLESSING OIL

2 ounces olive oil
2 tablespoons hyssop
9 drops sandalwood
9 drops myrrh

If you prefer a tinted oil try adding yellow food coloring one drop at a time until you achieve the desired color. Other good additives to this oil would be plant parts.

SANTA MUERTE DOMINATION OIL

2 ounces olive oil
2 tablespoons asafoetida
9 drops bistort

If you prefer a tinted oil try adding red food coloring one drop at a time until you achieve the desired color. Other good additives to this oil would be plant parts.

SANTA MUERTE CONTROLLING OIL

2 ounces olive oil
2 tablespoons damiana
2 tablespoons cinquefoil

If you prefer a tinted oil try adding red food coloring one drop at a time until you achieve the desired color. Other good additives to this oil would be plant stems, chips.

SANTA MUERTE HEALING OIL
2 ounces olive oil
2 tablespoons lavender
9 drops eucalyptus oil
9 drops hyssop oil
If you prefer a tinted oil try adding blue food coloring one drop at a time until you achieve the desired color. Other good additives to this oil would be eucalyptus twigs.

SANTA MUERTE SUCCESS OIL
2 ounces olive oil
2 tablespoons irish moss
1 tablespoon juniper
If you prefer a tinted oil try adding yellow or green food coloring one drop at a time until you achieve the desired color. Other good additives to this oil would be juniper berries.

SANTA MUERTE DARK ART OIL
2 ounces olive oil
2 tablespoons knotweed
If you prefer a tinted oil try adding blue, green, and red food coloring one drop at a time until you achieve an almost black color. Other good additives to this oil would be hemlock or wormwood pieces.

SANTA MUERTE COMMANDING OIL
2 ounces olive oil
2 tablespoons elder
9 drops patchouli oil
If you prefer a tinted oil try adding blue, green, and red food

coloring one drop at a time until you achieve an almost black color. Other good additives to this oil would be pieces of devils shoestring.

SANTA MUERTE COURT OIL

2 ounces olive oil
2 tablespoons galangal
9 drops bergamot oil

If you prefer a tinted oil try adding blue or yellow food coloring one drop at a time until you achieve the desired color. Other good additives to this oil would be pieces of nutmeg, or high John chips.

SANTA MUERTE EMPLOYMENT OIL

2 ounces olive oil
2 tablespoons wahoo
9 drops sandalwood oil

If you prefer a tinted oil try adding blue, yellow, or green food coloring one drop at a time until you achieve the desired color. Other good additives to this oil would be pieces of cinnamon stick.

SANTA MUERTE BREAK UP OIL

2 ounces olive oil
2 tablespoons cayenne
1 tablespoon henbane

If you prefer a tinted oil try adding blue, green, and red food coloring one drop at a time until you achieve a blackish color. Other good additives to this oil would be pieces of broken glass or hair from a black dog.

SANTA MUERTE DRESSING POWDERS

The base for all these powders is talc and/or cornstarch. To make the powders place all your ingredients in a mortal and pestle including any oils that are added. Then grind well, incorporating all the ingredients together.

Santa Muerte Attraction Powder

2 tablespoons jasmine
1 tablespoon cyclamen
1 tablespoon sandalwood or 9 drops in oil form

Santa Muerte Wisdom Powder

2 tablespoons crushed rose petals
1 tablespoon elder

Santa Muerte Better Business Powder

2 tablespoons oakmoss
1 tablespoon cinnamon

Santa Muerte Black Art Powder

2 tablespoons gum mastic
1 tablespoon ambergris

Santa Muerte Invoking Powder

2 tablespoons copal resin
1 tablespoon elder

Santa Muerte Commanding Powder

2 tablespoons licorice root
1 tablespoon fennel

Santa Muerte Money Powder

2 tablespoons frankincense
1 tablespoon Cinnamon
9 drops hyssop oil

Santa Muerte Good Luck Powder

2 tablespoons arrow root

1 tablespoon allspice

Santa Muerte Separation Powder
2 tablespoons asafoetida
1 tablespoon vetivert

Santa Muerte Get Away Powder
2 tablespoons cayenne
1 tablespoon sulfur

Santa Muerte Confusion Powder
2 tablespoons barberry
1 tablespoon figwort

Santa Muerte Court Case Powder
2 tablespoons cascara sagrada
1 tablespoon buckthorn
1 tablespoon tobacco

Santa Muerte Love Powder
2 tablespoons crushed rose petals
1 tablespoon cassia

Santa Muerte Prosperity Powder
2 tablespoons goldenseal
1 tablespoon clove

SIMPLE AND EFFECTIVE WAYS TO CAST STRONGER, LONGER LASTING SPELLS

Here are some tips to making your spellwork stronger acting and longer lasting. The extra work involved makes the difference in a weak outcome and an outcome with a

BANG!

Cleansings

The effects of a good thorough cleansing can have such a great impact on spellwork. In my opinion its one of the most important beginning and ending steps that one can take to influence a positive and desirable outcome. Use whatever method of cleansing you normally would, just don't skip it altogether and don't rush the cleansing process. Cleanse, cleanse, and cleanse in order to clear away negativities, to make yourself, your space, and the tools you use pure and fit for the spiritual work ahead. Cleanse in the beginning and at the end of a job. Why start a job with obstacles in the beginning and why end a job with unneeded energies right?

Meditate

People often associate meditation with long periods of sitting cross-legged on the floors chanting "OM". This is not always the case. The fact is you can spend as little as 10 minutes in a meditative state and still greatly gain from it. Meditation trains the mind. Not only is there health benefits that can be gained from it but it also enables us to focus, concentrate, visualize, and connect. All the things needed in spiritual work. Meditation reaches far within, beyond the conscious and subconscious mind and begins drawing on the finer energies that reside at the deeper levels of the super-conscious mind. Here there is an infinite source of energy. In meditative states we are aware and able to receive messages from other realms. It sharpens our inner vision and multiplies our inner hearing. Meditation conditions the mind to become more receptive to information. In spellwork meditation, visualization, and intention are used to direct the energy of spells.

Mental Imaging/Visualization

Creative visualization is the art of changing negative

thinking for positive images and creating what we desire. Some know this as manifestation. By thinking of the good things you want to happen as part of a regular routine, you're creating a positive energy. Instead of observing a situation you want changed, visualize the situation as you want it to be. The mind produces some of the most powerful energy known. When we visualize something, we are creating a new energy. In spellwork the most critical tool you have at your disposal is your mind. Just like any other tool it requires maintenance to keep it in shape. The power of your spellwork is a reflection of your spiritual strength.

Personal Concerns

Personal concerns, items that personally belong or come from the person on whom spellwork is intended for, empowers a spell. The more personal items you have, the stronger the connection. These items enliven the spellwork at hand, gives dimension, and fills it with the life essence of the target person. If you have access to personal items its worth the time and effort to collect them. Some items which as powerful in spellwork include things such as hair (from any part of the body), unwashed clothing, and body fluids. You could probably come up with a lot more if you think about it. When searching for personal items try looking in odd places such as a hairbrush (hair), trash cans (hair, body fluids on paper), sheets (hair, skin), hats (hair), etc.

Symbolism

Don't forget to add some items that are symbolic of your desired outcome. These can be trinkets or printed images. For instance, it you are working a money drawing spell try including images of money bags or printed hundred bills. For love related work you could include images of happy couples or hearts. If your goal is for marriage to take place include pictures of a bride and groom, an engagement ring,

Santa Muerte: Altars, Offerings Prayers, & Spells

or a wedding ceremony. For prosperity spells or to remove
obstacles try small pad locks (leave them open, not locked)
or keys. Use your imagination.

Moon Phase
For those who aren't heavily in to incorporating
planetary aspects into spellwork a very simple and quick
method is to begin spellwork by the moon phases. Just
remember that when the goal of the spell is to remove, rid,
shrink, or send something away begin the work during the
waning moon phase. When the goal of the spell is to attract,
bring, grow, or increase something begin the work during
the phase of the waxing moon.

Faith/Think Positive
In all spellwork having faith is of great importance.
Don't allow negative thinking to come in to play. Believe
that your spell will work to your desired outcome. If a
negative thought presents itself chase it away immediately.
Thinking negatively only weakens you.